AfterNow

what next for a healthy Scotland?

Phil Hanlon &
Sandra Carlisle

ARGYLL ✠ PUBLISHING

Argyll Publishing
Glendaruel
Argyll PA22 3AE

www.argyllpublishing.co.uk
www.afternow.co.uk
www.centreforconfidence.co.uk
www.postcardsfromscotland.co.uk

The authors have asserted their moral rights.

British Library Cataloguing-in-Publication Data.

A catalogue record for this book is available from the British Library.

ISBN 978 1 908931 05 4

Printing
Martins the Printers, Berwick upon Tweed

AfterNow

previous books by the authors

Hanlon P, Carlisle S, Hannah M and Lyon A.
The Future Public Health
Open University Press (2012)

CONTENTS

Acknowledgements 9

1. Warning lights on the dashboard 11

2. The 'Scottish effect' – a warning light 17

3. 'Dis-ease' in Scotland 27

4. Loss of well-being 43

5. Why change is inevitable 57

6. Who is showing the way? 75

7 What next for a healthy Scotland? 101

'. . . the values of modernity – materialism, individualism, consumerism, scientism and economism – have a considerable hold on our society and our leaders. Like the frog sitting in water slowly being heated to boiling point, we seem oblivious to the malign effects of this environment.'

ACKNOWLEDGEMENTS

This book derives from work originally funded by the Scottish Government on the relationship between 'modern' culture and well-being – the AfterNow project. We thank Geoff Huggins, Head of the Mental Health Division of the Scottish Government, for his support. We have also been supported by the Glasgow Centre for Population Health: we are grateful to its Director Professor Carol Tannahill and David Walsh (David's research features in Chapter 2).

Thanks are due to members of our research steering group, in particular, Dr David Reilly, of the NHS Centre for Integrative Care in Glasgow, whose inspirational work in reorienting medical care has informed our thinking over many years.

International Futures Forum, based in Scotland, has also provided a source of fresh thinking on the 'change of age' now facing humanity. Their contribution to this work is not so much in this or that aspect of the arguments we set out, but rather in the way that the whole problem is seen. We would like to acknowledge, in particular, Andrew Lyon, Graham Leicester, Tony Hodgson and Maureen O'Hara. We are also grateful to Margaret Hannah, Deputy Director of

Public Health in NHS Fife, who has been learning closely with IFF for many years and has been a collaborator on the AfterNow project.

Finally, Phil would like to acknowledge the contribution of his wife, Lesley, who has spent many hours discussing these issues with him and contributed substantially to aspects of the work when they undertook a joint sabbatical.

CHAPTER ONE

Warning lights on the dashboard

Imagine that you are on a road trip into the wilderness. Darkness is falling, the last garage was passed ten miles back, your driver seems lost and the road ahead leads deeper into the desert. Then the temperature warning light on the dashboard begins to flash. Your driver finds a sticking plaster, places it over the red light and mutters 'that's better!' How worried would you be? To press on at night, unsure of where you are going, and with a malfunctioning car, seems foolhardy. When the temperature gauge starts flashing, surely any sensible driver would stop the car and try to find the cause of the problem rather than cover the warning light with a sticking plaster. In this book we argue that warning lights are flashing for Scotland. We see them but we are not responding appropriately. If we were to discern their significance, it would open up the possibility of a better future for all of us. After all, Scotland is a country with an extraordinary history of achievement, a resourceful people and many natural advantages. Yet, our current trajectory is leading us into great peril.

This book is underpinned by findings, insights and thinking

derived from a six year research programme on well-being in Scotland – the AfterNow project. Our professional backgrounds are in public health and there is much about the health of Scotland in this book. However, the themes we explore are wider than health and relevant to all.

Nevertheless, given that we begin our analysis with the health of Scotland, we suggest three reasons why the Scottish people should pay more attention to this aspect of our current predicament. First, health is a resource for living: many in Scotland suffer ill health when our counterparts in similar countries do not and this state of affairs needlessly robs many Scots of opportunities in life. Second, health is a key dimension of resilience – that is, the ability to bounce back after a setback. So, when we observe that health in Scotland is poor, it means that our population may not be as resilient as it needs to be to cope with some of the challenges we anticipate coming our way in the near future. Third, the health of a population is an excellent barometer of how well things are going in that society. This is because the health of a population is the product of cumulative interactions over the life course of many important factors, including the physical environment, the social environment, prosperity, equity, health-related behaviours like smoking, diet and exercise, employment, education, service provision and much else. So, if health is poor, it suggests that all may not be well in our society.

For these reasons, Scotland's continuing poor health status should be a clear warning light. It should cause us to take action – not just on health but on the many factors that contribute to our poor health. The political response is usually

'Scotland's health is improving – just not quickly enough'. There is, of course, truth in this statement and the last thing we want to do is engage in a pessimistic 'glass half empty' analysis. The point we want to make is that Scotland's current health trajectory tells us something important about our whole way of life and our prospects for the future.

The health problems which are of greatest immediate concern – and constitute a clear warning light for Scotland – are of a different nature to those we have successfully overcome in the past. We believe they are cultural as much as structural or material in origin and character. They are, for example, the emerging 'epidemics' of obesity and problematic drug and alcohol use. In Scotland, we have strikingly high rates of these consumption related problems compared to many similar countries. Why does Scottish society have such a severe manifestation of these modern epidemics? We might call such problems 'dis-eases' (rather than diseases). They reflect an 'inner world' – the realm of our individual consciousness, beliefs and motivations – that is struggling to cope with modern life.

We argue in more detail later that these dis-eases are a product of late modernity. That is, they are an emergent consequence of the very nature of the lives we have created for ourselves. If this is true (and readers should reserve judgement till the full arguments are set out) problems like obesity, inequality or loss of well-being cannot be fixed by conventional policy interventions. More profound, more integral and embodied change will be needed. Is there any convincing evidence that we have the will to achieve such profound change? Not yet. However, there are good reasons to be hopeful because we have been in this type of situation before. With the benefit of hindsight, we can identify a number of 'ages', each with a distinctive outer world (social structure, economy, ecology and culture) and inner worlds (belief, motivation, consciousness). At the time, most people did not recognise what we are calling the outer and inner world – they just lived their lives. However, disruptions happened, usually due to resource and population pressures, and this catalysed a 'change of age'. To cope, our ancestors developed and integrated new outer worlds (technologies, social systems and cultures) and inner worlds (beliefs, consciousness). The modern age followed this pattern. Resource and population pressures catalysed change and, over an extended period, our modern world emerged.

'Modernity' is the term we are using to describe the period of time since the Enlightenment: one that has been character-ised by a distinctive and integrated inner and outer world. The inner world of modernity has taught us to think of ourselves as complex biological machines that are the product of chance and time. We understand ourselves as individuals, subject to biological competition (survival of the fittest) and social competition (the market). The outer world of modernity is dominated by materialism, individualism, consumerism and economism. We understand the world both as a resource to be used and a complex machine that needs managing. We accept that the task of an organised society is to satisfy the inexorable, growing needs of the human population.

We know that the contemporary social, political, cultural and economic context in which we live has provided many benefits: for example, freedom of choice, individual rights, better health and social conditions and higher levels of material comfort for many. The point is that these considerable gains have not been achieved without equally considerable costs. One of the most significant of these costs, in terms of population health, appears to be static or declining levels of well-being for individuals, a rise in rates of mental health problems and disorders, and an accompanying rise in new forms of social problems. Yet, most of the contemporary solutions offered for the dis-eases of modernity have virtually no chance of working, because they are rooted in the ways of thinking, being and doing of modernity. If the root of the problem is modernity, then modernity is unlikely to provide the answer.

However, we will argue that profound change now appears inevitable because our way of living is not sustainable – ecologically, economically or emotionally. Therefore, if change is forced upon us, this opens up the possibility of creating a better future – one where we have truly addressed problems like inequalities and loss of well-being.

We can be confident that profound change is inevitable because exponential growth (which is intrinsic to the current mindset and economic system) cannot continue indefinitely in a finite system (the natural limitations of our planet). Unfortunately, as humans, we are extremely poor at appreciating the dynamics of exponential growth. As a result, we tend to ignore the certainty of in-built collapse in any finite system that pursues such unsustainable growth patterns. Three key areas are currently growing exponentially: all three are linked to the exponential expansion in human numbers and the escalating resource use of human societies. These linked phenomena are energy, the economy and the environment.

Scotland was one of the epicentres of the Enlightenment and, as such, helped to create the modern world and contributed much to our modern scientific understanding and technological advances. As modernity comes to an end, an analogous act of invention is needed to help create a better and more sustainable future. In this book we argue that the problems that currently beset Scotland are simply a more virulent manifestation of symptoms that are indicative of modernity in decline or transition. The fact that we have such a florid manifestation of the dis-eases of modernity provides us with an opportunity, once again, to be an epicentre of a new enlightenment which could illumine our path into the future. Over the course of the following chapters we lay out the complex and inter-related nature of the challenges we face and propose how we might best respond.

Finally, to keep the book short and accessible to general readers we have omitted references. We have compiled a list of data sources and relevant publications and they are available on the website which accompanies this series.[1]

[1.] Please go to the AfterNow section of
www.postcardsfromscotland.co.uk

CHAPTER TWO

The 'Scottish effect' – a warning light

If the countries that make up the United Kingdom were regarded as separate entities, then life expectancy in Scotland would, for men and women, be the lowest in the European Union. Scotland is only now achieving levels of life expectancy seen in the best performing European countries in 1970. Yet Scotland has not always performed so poorly. In the first half of the twentieth century life expectancy in Scotland was actually higher for both men and women than in other Western European countries such as France, Spain and Italy. In the mid-twentieth century however, while other countries (many of which had once lagged behind Scotland) improved, Scotland began to slip down the table of European life expectancy. That is why the usual political response to these data – 'Scotland's health is improving: only not fast enough' – is accurate. In recent decades Scotland has, indeed, suffered a relative decline in life expectancy while improving in absolute terms. We are so used to considering Scotland the 'sick man of Europe' that we are prone to think 'well, what else can we expect?' Yet Scotland is a rich country: richer than many regions of the UK and several of the countries of

Europe that outstrip us in health. Why should Scotland 'punch below its weight' in health outcomes?

To understand this, it is necessary to look at differences in deaths at different ages, among men and women, and from different causes. This shows that Scotland's position is not exceptional in infant and childhood mortality. At older ages, while worse than the European average, it is not the worst. Instead, Scotland's overall poor position is driven, to a considerable extent, by the very high mortality of working age adults, where both men and women lag well behind European counterparts. The most frequently cited reason for this pattern in Scotland's poor health is post-industrial decline, accompanied by all the manifestations of socio-economic deprivation that go with it, especially unemployment. Part of the evidence to support this theory comes from the observation that, within Scotland, the poorest health is found in the West-Central belt, a region that experienced the effects of profound deindustrialisation in recent decades.

However, other parts of the UK and Western Europe have also suffered deindustrialisation and are similarly characterised by social deprivation, unemployment and relative poverty. So, by making comparisons between Scotland and these other deindustrialised areas, it should be possible to discover whether they too experienced adverse health effects and how they compare to Scotland, particularly West-Central Scotland. In research conducted by the Glasgow Centre for Population Health (GCPH), ten regions were selected for analysis: the Ruhr area and Saxony in Germany; Katowice in Poland; Northern Moravia in the Czech Republic; Nord-Pas-de-Calais in France; Wallonia in Belgium; Limburg in the Netherlands; Northern Ireland; Swansea and the South Wales

coalfields in Wales; and Merseyside in England. The investigation found that post-industrial decline in all countries is
associated with lower levels of prosperity and higher mortality.
All the post-industrial regions examined had poor health and
social outcomes compared to their respective national
averages. However, mortality rates of comparable, post-
industrial regions elsewhere in Europe are *improving at a
faster rate* than the West of Scotland. At the same time, the
West of Scotland's current economic status is *better* than most
of the other regions. This is particularly true when Scotland
is compared to countries in Eastern Europe. Scotland is
wealthier than places like Poland and the Czech Republic but
health in their post-industrial regions is improving more
rapidly.

So, we are confronted by a conundrum. Scotland is a
wealthy Western European country that seems to be performing less well than it should in heath outcomes. We blame
deprivation and post-industrial decline but these factors,
while important, do not seem to be the complete answer.
The term 'Scottish Effect' has been coined as shorthand for
this unexplained excess mortality occurring in Scotland (and
in particular the West of Scotland), after the effect of
deprivation has been taken into account. A group of researchers, including the authors of this book, associated initially
with the Public Health Institute of Scotland and latterly with
the Glasgow Centre for Population Health (GCPH) have
explored the 'Scottish effect' and its main component, the
'Glasgow effect'. David Walsh of the GCPH has led much of
this work – in particular, an elegant comparison of three cities:
Glasgow, Liverpool and Manchester. The results are remarkable.

Liverpool and Manchester are two cities which stand out

because they share with Glasgow high levels of poverty and low life expectancy. Indeed, when the deprivation profiles of the three cities are analysed, there is almost no difference. This means that any difference observed in health outcomes cannot be explained by deprivation because all three manifest the same levels of deprivation. Importantly, before this work was carried out, no differences in mortality would have been anticipated between three such similar cities. In the event, the data were clear. Working aged adults in Glasgow have 30% higher mortality than in the two English cities. Also, excess mortality for Glasgow, relative to Liverpool and Manchester, can be seen across the whole population, with all age mortality around 18% higher in the most deprived decile but also 15% higher in the least deprived decile.

Since this is such a surprising result we need to be absolutely clear about what this means: currently, there are 15% more deaths in *affluent* areas of Glasgow like Bearsden or Newton Mearns compared to similarly affluent neighbourhoods in Manchester or Liverpool. Also, similar levels of like-for-like excesses in mortality can be found across all social groups.

What are the causes of death that contribute most to this 'Glasgow effect'? That graph opposite sets out the details. Remember that these are like-for-like comparisons, and that traditional wisdom would have led us to expect no important differences between equally deprived cities. Yet, for both cancers and diseases of the circulatory system Glasgow has 12% more deaths. Deaths among Glaswegians (relative to residents of Liverpool and Manchester) are 27% higher in relation to lung cancer, while smoking rates are almost identical. Glasgow's rates are 32% higher for external causes and almost 70% higher for suicide. These results are concern-

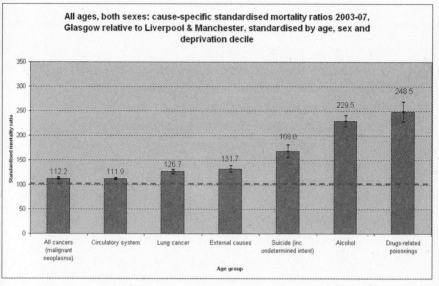

All ages, both sexes: cause-specific standardised mortality ratios 2003-07, Glasgow relative to Liverpool & Manchester, standardised by age, sex and deprivation decile

ing enough but the excess deaths due to alcohol and drugs are the most shocking. Glasgow has death rates that are 2.3 times higher for alcohol-related causes, and almost 2.5 times higher for drug-related poisonings. The numbers of deaths involved are large. Between 2003 and 2007 there were more than 4,500 'excess' deaths in Glasgow, of which almost half (2,090) occurred under the age of 65. Analysis by age, sex and cause shows that, for deaths under 65, almost half of the excess was due to deaths from a combination of alcohol-related causes (32%) and drugs related poisonings (17%).

There is evidence to suggest that this unexplained excess – the Glasgow effect – is a relatively recent phenomenon. Analyses of historical data suggest it is unlikely that the deprivation profile of Glasgow has changed significantly relative to Liverpool and Manchester in recent decades. However, the mortality gap appears to have widened since the early 1970s. These results emphasise that while deprivation is a fundamental determinant of health and, therefore, an important driver of mortality, it is only one part of a more complex picture. As currently measured, deprivation does not explain the higher levels of mortality experienced by Glasgow (and for that matter the whole of Scotland: this explanation focuses on Glasgow because the differences are so dramatic but the effect is just as real throughout Scotland even if it is not so large). Additional explanations are required. The research team involved in the series of studies referred to above has tested possible explanations. However, each resulting academic paper has increased the sense of mystery around the effect by showing that it cannot be explained adequately by many of the factors usually considered by epidemiological approaches to population health.

At present we cannot be certain about the causes of the Scottish effect. Many hypotheses are actively being investigated including migration; differing health behaviours; divergent values and cultures; the influence of cultures of substance misuse; boundlessness and alienation; family structures, gender relations and parenting differences; lower social capital; sectarianism; limited social mobility; health service supply or demand; deprivation concentrations, inequalities; patterns of deindustrialisation; political attack, and climatic differences (linked possibly to Vitamin D). To date, no single explanation has been found. For example, differences in health related behaviours and risks (like smoking, diet and blood pressure) do not, at least from the data currently available, explain the Scottish/Glasgow effect. A more social and historical approach may be needed to develop our understanding of why things are as they are, and to identify clues as to how they might be changed. An approach that blends history, culture, politics, literature, sociology, psychology and epidemiology may provide a set of insights that might explain more than any single disciplinary approach has achieved.

This has been the approach taken by the AfterNow project and this book sets out our thinking. At this stage, we will simply dip into two lines of thought to illustrate the approach. Currently, economic inequalities are no worse in Scotland than in England – although the UK is a more economically unequal society than much of the rest of Europe. Therefore, the Scottish effect cannot be easily explained by current levels of inequality. Nonetheless, insights can be gained from Neil Ascherson's historical concept of the 'St Andrew's Fault', which helps explain the emergence of an unhealthy split in Scottish society, between rich and poor and the confident minority and the mistrustful majority. These insights link into the work of social epidemiologist Richard Wilkinson, whose work integrates empirical observations with theories about psycho-social mechanisms underpinning health inequalities. Wilkinson's thinking seems to be increasingly shifting towards a focus on the relationship between emotional/mental well-being and physical health: he argues that it is not just what your material circumstances do to your health directly which matters, but also what your social position makes you feel about your circumstances.

Wilkinson and Pickett's highly influential book, *The Spirit Level,* shows that, once a country becomes sufficiently wealthy to demonstrate reasonable levels of health, additional improvements in national wealth (GNP) are not associated with equivalent improvements in life expectancy (and a variety of other health and social outcomes). Indeed, the ranking of life expectancy amongst the developed countries of the world shows surprising results. The best predictor of life expectancy is not national wealth but the Gini co-efficient. The Gini co-efficient is sometimes called the 'Robin Hood index', because it measures income inequality. What this work shows is that wealthy countries with fairer distributions of income within the population enjoy higher life expectancy (and other positive health and social outcomes) than countries with an equivalent level of GDP but less even distributions of income and wealth. Wilkinson argues that the gradient of income influences health through psycho-social effects: that is, it is bad for the health of the whole population to live in a society which is very unequal.

These insights can be linked to the work of French sociologist Pierre Bourdieu, arguably one of the key thinkers of the twentieth century. Bourdieu suggests that there are implications for health and well-being in terms of how meaning is constructed in society, and how this determines behaviour, in the apparently routinised understandings and mundane activities of everyday life. Bourdieu's concept of the *habitus* plays a crucial role in accounting for the unthinking nature of most human action. The *habitus* can be crudely explained as the mental structure through which people deal with their day-to-day world: it can be thought of as a set of internalised schemes through which the world is perceived and acted on. It is formed in the context of people's specific social position, inculcates them into a world view which is based on that position and thus serves to reproduce existing social structures. It is class-dependent yet provides seemingly naturalised ways of thinking, feeling, acting and classifying the social world and one's location within it. As a result, people may have the capacity to change their lifestyles but will not necessarily be disposed or motivated to do so. Changes that do occur will tend to be in accordance with their underlying *habitus*.

Bourdieu points out that 'investing' in the control and development of the body and the self (as important sites of health and well-being) is a particular form of social practice unlikely to be evenly distributed across society. Put bluntly, eating 'healthily', taking physical exercise, learning to relax through meditation, and a whole range of other similar behaviours are unlikely to be part of the *habitus* or disposition of less advantaged groups. Conversely, groups high in cultural and educational capital are able to practice a key form of social distinction in contemporary society through extensive investments of this type. The utility for public health is that *habitus* is not an abstract concept: it only exists in the concrete practices of real people. We can, therefore, speculate that there are aspects of the *habitus* of various social groupings in Scotland which help to explain differences between social groups within Scotland. It is also possible that the *habitus* of people throughout Scotland has developed features in recent decades that might explain the Scottish effect.

The argument here is not simply that we are not in a position, as yet, to define these differences (and thus explain the Glasgow/Scottish effect). Rather, the argument is that Scotland's poor health is likely to be the complex product of structural, cultural and behavioural factors that have emerged in recent decades. This is a key part of the overall argument. Our culture and our social structure interact with our inner world (world view) to influence both our biology and our behaviour, in a way that manifests itself as health or illness. Thus, the patterns of health and illness in Scotland may be telling us something important about our whole society.

'. . . these problems (obesity and alcohol) are emergent manifestations of our modern way of life: they reflect our modern, competitive society and all its discontents, and they are a consequence of the inner and outer worlds that we have created.'

CHAPTER THREE

'Dis-ease' in Scotland

There are several important examples of the ways in which our social structures and cultural systems have interacted with our inner world and our biology to influence health and disease. In this chapter we will explore two of the most marked: obesity and problematic alcohol use. We have chosen these examples from many possible others because each is getting worse and is causing increased human suffering and adding to the mounting burden shouldered by the NHS. We begin by asking why we find this sort of problem so difficult to combat? In some ways it is a surprise, given our success in other areas. Infectious diseases have been controlled and many of the major killers of the twentieth century have responded to public health interventions. Yet, despite our best efforts, problems caused by obesity and alcohol are getting worse. The reason seems to be that these problems are emergent manifestations of our modern way of life: they reflect our modern, competitive society and all its discontents, and they are a consequence of the inner and outer worlds that we have created.

We begin by examining the obesity epidemic. Obesity is a condition characterised by an excess of body fat. There are a variety of ways in which obesity can be assessed in individuals and populations. One commonly used definition of obesity is the *Body Mass Index* (BMI), which is a person's weight in kilograms divided by the square of their height in metres. For adults, overweight is defined as a BMI of greater than 25 and obesity is defined as a BMI of greater than 30. This is not without its problems, as an athlete with a large muscle bulk can have a high BMI but not be obese. However, as a tool to assess levels of obesity in populations, it is fit for purpose.

America led the world's obesity epidemic and where America leads many countries have followed: Scotland is leading the chasing pack. Almost two thirds of the Scottish population (65%) are either overweight or obese and more than a quarter of adults in Scotland are obese: specifically, 27% of Scots between the ages of 16 and 64 were obese in 2010. Projections suggest that adult obesity in Scotland couldreach 40% by 2030. We call it an epidemic because there has been a marked increase in the occurrence of obesity, not because there is any contagion. It is an epidemic that has unfolded over the last three to four decades. Scottish Health Survey data show that the levels in 2010 (27% obesity) are up from just 17% in 1995 and, more importantly, adult rates of obesity were negligible (approximately 3%) as recently as the early 1970s. Why has Scotland moved from having trivial levels of obesity in the 1960s to a position where we have the second highest level of obesity in the developed world?

To help answer this question we need to look at the pattern of weight gain across the whole population. For example, if we examine the changing distribution of body mass index in Greater Glasgow we find that over the past two decades a growing proportion of people fall above the cut-off level at which obesity is defined: there are more obese people. However, the reason is that the distribution of BMIs in the whole population is moving to the right. What this means is that the entire population (or, to be more accurate, almost all the population) is involved in a pattern of weight gain. So, the slim are becoming less slim while those who are fat are getting fatter. There are individuals who buck this trend but they are a small proportion of the total.

In Scotland, this shift in the distribution of BMIs is caused by a one kilogram increase in weight, per adult, per year. This is an average figure across the whole population: some will gain much more and others less or none. The point is that one kilogram is just over two pounds, which does not seem like a massive yearly weight gain. The dynamic of the epidemic is better understood, however, when one realises that 1 kg each year translates into 10kg or 22lbs each decade. The average gain of one kilogram of body fat a year represents an additional 9,000 calories of stored energy. This gain is created by an average daily imbalance of just 25 calories a day – or less than one digestive biscuit! (Importantly, staying in balance most of the year and overeating on holidays and at Christmas can have the same effect).

So, a key dimension of the obesity epidemic in Scotland is being caused by quite small imbalances in energy over almost all the population. The argument which has just been set out is based on a very simple 'calories in minus calories out = weight balance' formula. However, evidence is accumulating to suggest that we need to consider the types of food we eat as well as simply counting calories. The sort of food we have moved towards are those that put the body into fat storage mode – so that for the same intake of calories, these products put on more weight than would have been the case if we ate what might be better called real or more natural foods. Again, this shift in food type has happened in almost all of the Scottish population.

The implication is clear. If we want to counter the obesity epidemic, we need to move the whole curve back to the left. Simply concentrating on those who are obese will not solve the problem. Changes involving almost the whole population have created the problem so it will take *population-wide change* to solve the problem.

In its simplest terms, obesity can be considered as an imbalance between the amount of energy consumed in the diet and the amount of energy expended through exercise and bodily functions. The relative importance of changes in energy intake (eating) and energy expenditure (physical activity) in driving the epidemic of obesity on a population level is unclear and may vary between countries. Much of the discourse about obesity focuses on self control in individuals. This creates the impression that the problem is caused by the behaviour of individuals who simply need to 'get a grip'. This approach is usually not helpful for individuals but it is simply misleading as a way of thinking about the obesity epidemic in whole populations. It is simply not plausible that, for the whole of human history, the human race avoided an obesity epidemic then, in the 1980s, collectively lost self control. The last thing most people want is to be obese. It is illogical to assume people have made themselves obese simply through being greedy or lazy.

The point is that throughout human history there have been individuals who were obese but they were the exception. In Scotland, today, being overweight has become the norm and obesity is the condition of a very large minority. The number of people who are overweight and obesity is both unprecedented and recent. Why has it happened? Our physiology was formed a long time ago when food was scarce and we needed large amounts of energy in order to find food and stay alive. Our ancestors are estimated to have expended about 1000 kilocalories per day in physical activity. Human beings adapted to these circumstances by eating food whenever it was available and conserving energy by moving only when necessary. This strategy of storing and conserving energy made perfect sense at the time. Indeed, a hunter gatherer who did not follow this strategy was unlikely to survive. So, to put it crudely, we are the offspring of generations of people who have prioritised eating high calorie food and sitting on their backsides! This strategy makes much less sense now in a society where food is easily come by and the average sedentary person only needs to expend about 300 kilocalories per day in physical activity. We are stuck with the metabolic and behavioural legacy of our evolutionary history. What changed to make that legacy so problematical?

The answer is – a great deal. The UK government's Foresight project on the obesity epidemic famously produced a diagram to capture the factors involved in creating an environment that promotes obesity. It shows a blizzard of boxes, arrows and feedback loops. The message was clear: a massive number of interacting factors are involved. It is, therefore, not surprising that we should have problems coping with an environment that exerts constant pressure to increase energy intake and to decrease energy expenditure. Influences include: increased traffic hazards for walkers and cyclists, such that we use less energy in active commuting; reduced opportunities for recreational physical activity; increased sedentary recreation (multiple TV channels around the clock, computer games and so on); greater quantities and variety of energy-dense foods available; rising levels and increasingly persuasive means of promoting and marketing of energy dense foods; more frequent and widespread food purchasing opportunities; more use of restaurants and fast food outlets; larger portions of food offering better 'value' for money (e.g. BOGOF, or 'buy one get one free').

These and many more influences create our obesogenic environment and this is now overriding the biological regulatory mechanisms in more and more people. The intensity of this obesogenicity is currently increasing with the expansion of the market-driven food manufacturing system; one that is responsive only to price signals, and a physical environment increasingly created to suit the needs of continued economic growth as well as the values base of a consumerist society.

The most nutritious foods on the planet are those provided by nature, whereas the most profitable are those produced by food manufacturers. Eating manufactured food has meant we eat more sugar: refined sugar intake has escalated to the extent that Scots now consume around 1.6 pounds of sugar per week. Refined sugar represents so-called 'empty calories'

– that is, they provide energy but none of the other nutrients we require. On average, Scots consume 400 of these empty calories per day.

At the same time, the National Food Survey for 1974-2000 confirms that our consumption of the following 'real' foods went down: meat; eggs; butter; fresh potatoes; all vegetables; fresh green vegetables; and milk. In some cases, the reduction in the consumption of real food was dramatic. We eat half the number of eggs that we used to, and one fifth of the butter and whole milk. In contrast, consumption of the following foods has gone up: confectionery; fruit products (more than doubled); ice cream and ice cream products (nearly tripled); processed meat; processed milk; cereals and cereal products; processed vegetables; processed potatoes (oven chips etc) (nearly tripled) and soft drinks (consumption of soft drinks in the year 2000 was over five times the consumption in 1974).

So, the obesity epidemic has coincided with a reduction in consumption of raw and natural foods, which have been largely replaced by processed food. This has led to the observation that 'man is the only species clever enough to make his own food and stupid enough to eat it'.

Meantime, the diet industry has escalated. If you reduce your calorie intake so that less energy is being consumed, the body doesn't automatically raid its fat reserves: rather, it cuts back on the energy expended. If you eat less you go hungry, which slows the metabolism, increases the desire to consume energy and reduces the desire to expend energy. Most commonly, the eventual result of a diet is weight gain. In response, we try to eat less and so the cycle goes on. Sustained weight loss may be one of the biggest challenges that the human body can face, given that the body is wired to both store fat and conserve energy. We know that for women, for example, a diet of 1000 calories a day should result in a weight loos of 140lbs each and every year, regardless of starting weight. Yet, instead, experience shows they lose little or nothing – and put on weight when they can't stand the (near)starvation any longer and eat close to normal daily requirements!

The somewhat discouraging picture being painted here is of organisms (human beings) who find themselves in an affluent economy dominated by commercial interests that sell them high calorie processed foods which they consume in more and more circumstances. At the same time, much else in life conspires to reduce physical activity. When – as is almost inevitable – weight goes on, dieting aids and plans are sold to us – which often result in further weight gain. This combination of interacting influences has been called 'the obesogenic environment'. Given that Scotland has the second highest level of obesity in the developed world (after the USA) it suggests that we are afflicted with a particularly severe manifestation of this environment.

Obesity is not the only problem for which Scotland now has escalating rates. The same is true of drugs and alcohol. One of us has been involved in an 'Independent Enquiry into Drugs and Alcohol in Scotland' and much of what follows comes from the evidence submitted to that enquiry. The enquiry also focused on drugs and, while we confine our discussion here to alcohol, it is of interest that drugs are also a problem which was not at all serious in Scotland until recent decades. Indeed, the enquiry saw reports from the 1960s which stated that Scotland only needed to worry about occasional pockets of drug use. Yet, Scotland now has the sixth largest problem with illicit drug use in the world. No other comparable country is anywhere near as high in the rankings and we find ourselves sixth in the list behind Afghanistan, Iran, Mauritius, Costa Rica and Russia. Alcohol-related harm has also seen a dramatic increase in recent decades.

The year 1991 saw the beginning of a trend that has led to a nearly fourfold increase in male deaths and a doubling in female deaths from alcohol-related harm. The low level of deaths from alcohol in Scotland compared to Europe in the 1950s and 1960s should be noted. At that time our alcohol culture was based around males consuming beer in pubs. Alcohol-related problems existed but they were of a different nature and were not on the scale we face today. What has changed? This is best summarised in the answers to three questions: who drinks, what do they drink and where do they drink?

In the 1950s and 1960s, the alcohol culture was based around men who worked in manufacturing industries drinking in the pub. Today, if we ask who drinks, the answer is: virtually everybody. If we ask what they drink, the answer is a massive variety of different drinks. And if we ask where they drink, the answer is many different locations, including the home. In short, there has been a marked shift in Scotland's drinking culture. Finally, if we speculate as to why they drink, it seems logical to suggest that the *habitus* of many individual Scots and our wider collective culture has changed. The drinks industry and their advertising arm have played their part in this but we also need to look to a wider set of influences that cause us to seek pleasure as a substitute for deeper happiness and more profound purpose.

Evidence from younger people in Scotland suggests that, while there is no single experience, drinking for many starts at a very early age and young people increasingly 'drink to get drunk' (or wrecked/hammered – choose your own euphemism). Boredom is apparently a salient factor. Alcohol helps to fill time and makes social interaction easier. Because it is now so socially acceptable, drinking has become an increasingly popular recreational activity. Add to this the fact that alcohol is inexpensive, which makes it the cheap option, compared with other group activities. Alcohol also relieves stress and can be a means of escape from some of the less tolerable aspects of what, for some, may be difficult lives. Alcohol, particularly for younger teenagers, is a forbidden fruit and thus has a symbolic role in rebellion which drives some drinking behaviour. However, the main motivation for drinking does not seem to be rebellion or release from pain or anything else – it is simply normative. For many, drinking seems to be just what you do if you are young and live in Scotland. If you don't drink you can feel excluded. For most young people the dangers set out in health education messages do not seem real and are too far in the future to matter anyway.

For the whole population, alcohol is now cheaper and more widely available and evidence suggests that this is one key reason why it is now consumed in much larger quantities by a much wider range of age and social groups in Scotland. We agree that price and availability are key factors but also want to explore a deeper analysis.

One way of thinking about this is to use the metaphor of an iceberg in the surrounding ocean. The visible part of the iceberg above the surface of the water is made up of those who have an 'overwhelming involvement' with alcohol, to the extent that they are causing harm to themselves and/or others. But the bulk of the iceberg is hidden below the surface and represents alcohol use that is *not* visible, either because it is unproblematic or is being deliberately hidden. The surrounding ocean represents our culture: the way we raise our children; the competitiveness of our society and the stresses this induces; the unequal distribution of wealth and opportunity; the norms we create for behaviour; the price and availability of alcohol; the degree of mutual support we give to each other – and much else. We therefore need to give thought to what might 'raise the temperature' of the ocean and thus shrink the iceberg. One good place to start is to consider what has been happening in Scotland to *chill* our social waters and cause the iceberg to expand so dramatically.

It is surely of interest that, during the 1820s and 30s, when the industrial revolution was getting under way in Scotland and life was very hard for those who had been forced to migrate to cities like Glasgow, alcohol consumption was higher than it is today. Psychologist Bruce Alexander argues convincingly that we can best understand what happened in the disruption of rapid industrialisation as an *adaptation* to psychological distress created by social, cultural and economic circumstances. In other words, it is best seen as part of the way in which human populations have, throughout history, responded to social disruption and psychological dislocation. As the industrial revolution progressed, order became established and prosperity rose. People in Scotland derived a sense of purpose, meaning and belonging from family, church and work – maybe even from empire. Yet, at this time, Scotland was a low wage economy. Overcrowding in the home was a problem. As the twentieth century dawned, women and men pursued different arenas of what might be called 'social release' (men in the pub, women in the home and, where they could afford it, the cinema). Violence and sectarianism were never far under the surface. During this period, alcohol-related harm lessened but still remained high.

The post-war period was, in retrospect, highly conformist, relatively economically equal and a period of stability and political consensus. We are not arguing that this was any sort of golden age – for example, conformity made it a difficult time for many minority groups. However, in the post-war period, alcohol consumption was at a historically low level. It was still perceived to be a social (and moral!) problem but the levels of death and disease caused by alcohol were low. Deindustrialisation in places like West Central Scotland and Dundee changed the alcohol culture and also deprived many communities not just of jobs but also a sense of purpose and the social solidarity that goes with it. The role of family and community declined with the normative rise in importance of the individual and the desire to satisfy personal needs and wants. Furthermore, the gap between the incomes of the richest and poorest sections of our population widened.

Of course, these changes have also occurred in other countries. Yet, not all societies have responded to change by developing such high levels of drinking (and consequent alcohol-related harm). What we are suggesting here is that the deeper causes of Scotland's more recently difficult relationship with alcohol is an individualised, unequal, consumerist culture. We share this culture with many other countries but the evidence from the epidemics of alcohol-related harm suggests that Scotland has suffered a more extreme manifestation of these influences.

Lack of love and tenderness early in life may also be an important influence. The ACE (Adverse Childhood Experiences) study provides important evidence: children who are subject to adverse experiences in childhood are much more vulnerable during adolescence and adulthood. These adverse events include sexual, physical and verbal abuse, drugs and alcohol misuse in the home and a lack of love and encouragement. The converse is true: being loved unconditionally and supported by parents and others builds resilience in young people. Indeed, it might be argued that loving relationships of all sorts are a key factor in protecting individuals from falling into damaging interactions with drugs and alcohol and promoting recovery in those who have done so.

At several points in the Enquiry referred to above, evidence was presented that 'a common factor in successful recovery might best be summed up in a term we find it difficult to employ – spirituality'. The most important protection for young people against alcohol-related harm in the longer term is reported to be 'having purpose, meaning and a set of goals in their lives'. People who move into recovery often want to 'give something back' and 'become better than well'. This phenomenon is evident in '12 steps' programmes but is also frequently the key to successful recovery wherever it is found. However, we also heard that it is almost impossible to speak of these things in public organisations and official circles. In these contexts, it is seen as dangerous to speak of spirituality because it is so easily misheard as 'religion'. However, in the context of the recovery movement, the word spirituality refers not to a metaphysical proposition but to an observable human phenomenon which might be better termed a 'healing shift'.

What has been happening in the recovery movement in Scotland in the past few years is a source of enormous encouragement and hope. There is a 'healing shift' being observed in many lives; one that moves far beyond biology and behaviour to embrace values and relationships. There is no single language to describe the phenomenon but three key dimensions are usually present: a plausibility structure – a set of ideas that underpins recovery; a community of support; and an (often daily) practice to support the change. The phenomenology of the 'healing shift' is currently being observed in the recovery movement in Scotland but this is just one manifestation of something ubiquitous in human experience. The ability to mobilise a healing response, to grow as a person and transcend difficulties, is intrinsic to our humanity. It is part of many traditional religions and philosophies; fundamental to what we mean by 'art'; manifest in compassionate, person-centred health care and education; and is what we aspire to when we talk of 'assets based community development'. Indeed, it can probably be found wherever relationships lead to the mobilisation of inner resources.

On this basis it is plausible to argue that this 'healing shift' is not only needed by people in recovery but is also the very phenomenon which, if seen more widely in Scottish society, would 'raise the temperature of the water'. Yet the evidence from Scotland is that, for many, life seems difficult and mental health and well-being often suffers as a result. Understanding what modern life is doing to our sense of well-being is complex but its interpretation is important. We, therefore, will examine mental health and well-being in some detail in the next chapter.

'. . . the World Health Organisation is suggesting that, in the twenty-first century, depression and anxiety will become a far more significant cause of disability and chronic ill health than in previous centuries.'

CHAPTER FOUR

Loss of well-being

One of the most important manifestations of what we are calling dis-eases of modernity can be seen in mental health and well-being. However, unlike obesity or alcohol-related harm, data and information on mental health and well-being present us with far more complex issues of definition, measurement and diagnostic criteria. Definitions of, for example, depression encompass a range of elements which range from temporary low mood and sadness to prolonged and intense emotional disturbance and biomedical disorder. Also, depression is at least in part a socially and culturally constructed concept: the meaning and cultural significance of depression changes over time under the influence of market, professional, political and other forces. So, caution should be exercised in the interpretation of data.

The World Health Organisation (WHO) states that depression was the fourth leading contributor to the global burden of disease and disability in the year 2000 and will move up to second place by 2020. These predictions are uncertain but should not be discounted. This provides the most direct evidence of the degree to which modern populations are feeling overwhelmed. What the WHO is suggesting is that, in the twenty-first century, depression and anxiety will become a far more significant cause of disability and chronic ill health than in previous centuries. Some of this rise may be due to better detection, and some to modern protocol-driven diagnostic techniques. However, the general burden of stress, depression, anxiety and loss of well-being does seem to be rising and is being felt in many nations.

In Scotland, data show that the number and rates of hospital admissions and primary care consultations for depression appear to have reduced in recent years. Despite this apparent reduction, prescribing of antidepressants has increased from just over a million prescriptions in the early 1990s to nearly four million today. This may indicate that, in Scotland, depression has become subject to increasingly rigorous diagnostic criteria but at the same time, antidepressants are being prescribed to people who do not meet diagnostic criteria. This suggests that we may be medicating individuals who are suffering more from a loss of well-being than a clinically verifiable psychopathology.

So, there is an impression that mental health is deteriorating under modern pressures but proof of rising rates is limited by the lack of comparable datasets over time. This problem was addressed by researchers from the Medical Research Council's Public Health Sciences unit in Glasgow. Their results are remarkable.

Data were drawn from three comparable groups of 15 year olds in the West of Scotland for the years 1987, 1999 and 2006. Each sample was administered the same rigorous assessment, the 12-item General Health Questionnaire, which is a measure of self-reported psychological distress. The researchers assessed the level of 'caseness' which reflected levels of anxiety and depression, loss of confidence or self-esteem and social dysfunction. So, this study looked at comparable groups in the same location, assessed on each occasion with the same questionnaire. For boys, the levels of 'caseness' did not change much between 1987 and 1999 (13% and 15% respectively) but increased to 22% by 2006. For girls, the increases were much greater. 'Caseness' was 19% in 1987, 33% in 1999 and 44% in 2006. This means that nearly half of 15 year old girls reported sufficient psychological distress to meet the criteria for 'caseness'. The authors speculated that the increase in levels of psychological distress among young females over this period may be explained by an increase in educational expectations which, together with more traditional concerns about personal identity, appear to have elevated levels of stress, with adverse consequences for mental health. We have shown these data to males and females from senior school years in a number of locations across Scotland and none has expressed any surprise at the findings. When asked about likely causes, they speak of pressure to succeed, to look good, and to meet the expectations they feel parents, teachers and peers place upon them.

These results chime with what was discovered in a UNICEF child well-being report published in 2007. When compared with 20 other OECD countries, including substantially poorer ones, the UK was at the bottom of the league table of child well-being. The Netherlands headed the table of overall child well-being and Northern European countries, like Sweden, claimed the top four places. The United Kingdom and the

United States found themselves in the bottom third of the rankings for five of the six dimensions reviewed.

UNICEF UK commissioned Dr Agnes Nairn to explore some of the reasons behind these statistics by comparing children's experiences in the UK with those of children in Spain and Sweden. Nairn paid particular attention to the role of materialism and inequality in children's well-being. She found that family life in the three countries was strikingly different. In the UK, parents struggle to give children the time they clearly want to spend with them, whilst in Spain and Sweden family time is more woven into the fabric of everyday life. The roles played by mothers, fathers and children within the family and the rules which governed family life are much more clearly defined in Spain and Sweden than in the UK. She also found British families make less time for outdoor and creative activities amongst older and more deprived children.

Whilst most children agreed that family time is more important than consumer goods, Nairn observed within UK homes a compulsion on the part of some parents to continually buy new things both for themselves and their children. She tells us that 'boxes and boxes of toys, broken presents and unused electronics were witness to this drive to acquire new possessions, which in reality were not really wanted or treasured'. Most parents realised that what they were doing was often pointless but seemed pressurised and compelled to continue. She also noticed that UK parents were often buying their children status brands, believing that they were protecting them from the kind of bullying they experienced in their own childhood. This behaviour was largely absent in Spain and Sweden.

These findings echo much that we discovered through the AfterNow project. When we began to appreciate the scale of the damage being done by the dis-eases of modernity we imagined that, as more people began to appreciate the scale and nature of the problem, this alone might be sufficient to nudge the population in a new direction. We took our findings to a number of groups and individuals. We did this through what were called 'learning journeys', led by Andrew Lyon of the International Futures Forum (we will discuss the work of the International Futures Forum in more detail later). Our main question was the degree to which people living in Scotland perceive 'modern' culture to be a significant factor in their lives and circumstances, and how they articulated and responded to such trends. What was the influence of 'modern' culture on people's values, their beliefs and their views of the world?

We visited individuals and groups, in a range of contexts, whom we believed able to provide particular insight into this question. This work was supplemented by additional interviews with groups. In speaking to people drawn from a range of different socio-economic locations we found, without exception, that there is considerable interest in and appetite for debate around the issues outlined above. This confirmed our belief that such issues are both valid and important within contemporary Scottish lives. However, we found differences in the ways in which participants conceived and responded to modern culture. All agreed that individualism, materialism and the driving force of the market economy are forceful in contemporary lives but affluent participants tended to discuss in an abstract, impersonal, professionally contextualised way. Disadvantaged participants expressed far more personalised and critical views on the nature of modern life and its effects. Our sense is that the lives of more affluent participants were buffered by virtue of their more advantaged socio-economic position, together with their possession of substantial forms of economic, educational, social and cultural capital. Conversely, the excluded and stigmatised groups we spoke to seemed to have experienced the full force of the traits of modernity.

Senior academics spoke about the uncertainty of contemporary professional life within the accountability-driven domain of the public sector. We also heard of a gap between the ethos of the Scottish educational curriculum, which aims to support the well-being of young people through a broad-based education, and a broader culture that seems to squeeze out non-instrumental skills and values. In our interview with a secondary school head teacher, he observed that people everywhere live busy, consumer-driven lives. Their energies are devoted to money and mortgages. Their children are conscious of material wealth and that they have to work hard to get it. In such circumstances, education becomes a consumer product. The teacher observed that local parents, because of their own insecurities, bring an aggressive approach to their child's education: they know that educational qualifications are what allows individuals to make that step up. As a consequence, parents push for results and their children apparently share these views, becoming highly focused on success and material outcomes, to the exclusion of other aspects of their development.

The fast-paced, results-oriented business environment of a city call centre set up to service a large manufacturing industry provided a very different setting in which to explore our questions with others. We heard how the director of this private sector company sought to find ways of combating the dehumanising tendencies of a call centre environment. His approach involved giving staff intensive training plus some autonomy in addressing the problems and complaints of customers. These techniques enabled the company to achieve low rates of staff loss and high levels of customer satisfaction. Within the obvious limitations of the call centre environment, efforts to imbue otherwise deadening work with creativity and value appeared to be successful. However, although the call centre workers worked hard, they played hard too. Friday night binge-drinking is an entrenched part of young workers' lives on which company policies apparently have little impact. In our visit to a high-tech communications business, we heard from the general manager that his company seeks to give its employees the tools to manage their work-life balance through flexible working technology. However, well-being in this organisation had to be balanced with corporate pressures to do better, faster: as employee stress levels currently appear to be rising, the problem has not been solved.

The pervasive influence of consumer culture on individual, family, community and social well-being was powerfully voiced during our conversation with a group of male prisoners. One of our respondents suggested that contemporary culture influences well-being because it is profoundly isolating:

> People live in their own bubble, getting in their own car to drive to work, staying in their own home. Community spirit has gone and this compounds the issue. We're all in debt. You're stressed, you go to work, you go home. You sit in front of the TV. There's

> no family dinner, no time to talk problems through,
> sort things out. You're just working to afford that TV.
> There's no time for your children when you come
> home at night. No time to talk.   (Male prisoner)

One of his peers suggested that children are also under cultural pressure, not least because of media influence: he argued that there is now a greater divide between the haves and have-nots. Another suggested that 'capitalist society is about the stimulation of insecurity': a community that feels safe, for example, has less need to purchase insurance. People are driven, under such circumstances, to 'buy products and commodities to solve their perceived problems, such as cosmetic surgery'. Another man spoke of the enormous profits made by the large banking corporations who constantly attempt to get people to borrow money, 'offering credit through junk mail'. He suggested that there is 'real pressure to go into debt in order to have material things': young people, too, want the 'big house, flash car and plasma TV'. One argued that 'it's wider than just materialism. You want to do well and move on in order to get a better class of partner, a better standing in the community'.

Yet another concluded that:

> . . . our focus needs to go down to the spiritual – to
> the value and worth of a human being. Virtually
> nothing in society promotes that. We are exploitable
> because we are fearful. . . if you live in a society that's
> been founded on exploitation, how are you going to
> de-condition them? How do you make people feel
> more confident in themselves?

When we asked him what would help with this, he responded that we were all trapped in a cycle of consumerism and that powerful groups can't be expected to support anything that will counter techniques for maintaining social dominance.

We were told that people within the prison population and those in the housing estates outside tend to cope with the pressures of modern life through drug use. One man remarked on the presence of formal rites of passage in other cultures, which provide a sense of progression and development, and their absence from our own culture – as in the loss of the apprenticeship model for the non-academically inclined. All our society can provide, he suggested, are 'a series of transitions – from primary school to secondary school, and from there to further education, work, or the dole queue'.

Without romanticising the past, a variety of people we interviewed spoke of the erosion and decline of social, community and family support within contemporary Scottish society, together with the loss of stable and secure forms of employment: the result was just 'individuals living in the same space' rather than people able to connect with each other and 'pull together'. A key task perceived by some health and social care professionals was to prepare a third generation of people for survival in a life without work or wealth, in a context where they would be surrounded by those possessing both. It was bleakly observed that 'we live in a kind of very disposable economy, whether that be material things or even people.'

What we heard was that multiple – and compound – losses have been associated with social change over many decades. These changes were believed to impact on both individual and social levels of well-being. Social change is inextricably connected with cultural change. Those we spoke to acknowledged the psychological stresses and anxieties caused by increasing exposure to economic, status-related, consumerist imperatives. Our participants spoke of the pressures felt by people to define themselves through consumption practices, driven by life in a credit-and-debt culture.

A number of participants commented on the powerful influence of emotions like pride and shame. They spoke of people (including themselves, in some cases) being motivated by such emotions to buy material goods they could not really afford, simply in order to achieve a degree of social status. Worsening inequality was a matter of concern. Many believed that social divisions in contemporary society are widening, as the 'haves' leave disadvantaged people further and further behind and the social meanings created within consumer culture possess symbolic force which can add to wider inequalities.

So, our soundings from Scottish life (and we have only provided snippets from a much wider and richer dialogue) seem to confirm what various complex literatures are telling us. The modern world is one in which we can identify a prevailing ethos: materialism, consumerism, individualism, economism and an unshakable belief in the sustainability and desirability of economic growth.

Of course, no one subscribes to these values unquestioningly or unequivocally. The people we spoke to recognise the effects in themselves and others but did so with awareness. Nonetheless, it is easy to provide multiple examples or how these values are impacting on Scottish society. As we argued in the previous chapter, in the arena of public health we can see how these values impact. The obesity epidemic arises from a kaleidoscope of influences that we call the obesogenic society, the genesis of which can be traced back to increasing economic growth allied to economism and consumerism. The rise in alcohol-related harm in Scotland took off in the early 1990s when cost, availability and the drinking culture interacted to create the circumstances from which has emerged the alcohol harm epidemic – but all of that happened in a wider social and cultural context.

Yet, attempts to reverse these influences always encounter arguments based on economism and individualism. Out of town shopping developments are defended on the basis of economism and consumerism despite the social and health impacts that accompany them. Inequalities in Scotland are no longer driven by absolute poverty but by relative poverty and the exclusion of the poor from the choices that characterise the lives of those who are more affluent. Continuing economic growth simply widens inequalities. Why do we take this path?

Theories from the so-called new 'science of well-being' suggest that humans appear biologically designed to pursue social goals which may not be conducive to their long-term well-being. Thus, we adopt the social norms and behavioural strategies of those around us that ensure reproductive success and we feel good when pursuing such strategies successfully – social status, a professional career, 'positional goods' etc. However, because we are investing in sources of happiness which are intrinsically relative to what others have, this can result in escalating arms races where by definition only a few can succeed. Research confirms that we are *not* happy when those around us have more than we do. Our otherwise apparently irrational urge to stay on the hedonic treadmill and practise the relentless accumulation of 'positional goods' is thus explained by the positional psychology developed over human evolution.

We are not arguing that modern life is uniformly harmful to well-being. Yet, numerous social commentators have judged that aspects of contemporary culture are distinctively different from earlier forms and that their effects are perverse for both individual mental health and well-being, and for society. Participants in our discussions spoke of their aware-ness of socio-cultural trends towards greater individualisation in life, and increasing material and consumerist pressures. They also articulated their belief that the values underpinning such trends helped widen existing gaps between affluent and poor. Findings from this empirical work echo the arguments of numerous social theorists, in that participants located a contemporary sense of insecurity and social fragmentation in the weakening of institutions such as the family, the confusion wrought by economic dislocation, and changes in social cohesion.

This analysis also suggests that some contemporary problems can be located in the context of increasing social and individual disconnectedness and a widening gap between rich and poor. Participants noted that everyone in contemp-orary society is now exposed to unprecedented forms of consumerist pressures via mass marketing. The temptations of consumer culture were seen as an incentive to indebted-ness. They critiqued the dominance of economic values over personal and professional life, whilst stressing the importance of an adequate income to social inclusion and a sense of social respect. Nevertheless, they believed it not just possible but necessary to resist and re-think 'the disposable culture'.

Since consumerism as we now see it, only emerged during the mid-twentieth century, it is clear that there is no inherent impulse for consumerism in human nature. It was created to serve the needs of Western economies: consumerism emerged as the result of deliberate social engineering. Consumerism not only serves capitalism but also helps meet the (sometimes perverse) needs that capitalism creates – needs which are profoundly antithetical to human well-being. The capitalist system of production and consumption in modern western societies has resulted in widespread social change and the abandonment of traditional sources of meaning and social values. A sense of self and purpose in life is no longer ascribed, so that their development becomes a key task. Put simply, modernity is a recipe for identity crisis on a mass scale. Under these conditions, we are forced to construct our identity around the needs of the marketplace. With our identities largely constructed around consumption, the economic system exploits the very crisis that it creates by proffering its various goods as solutions. This leads to a general preoccupation with wealth, fame, physical appearance and material possessions at the individual level while economic growth and improvement in living standards becomes the preoccupation of our political system.

In the face of this critique, what do we observe in Scotland's largest city – Glasgow? In 2005 the city created a marketing campaign for itself entitled 'Glasgow – Scotland with style.' The tone and use of images is observably and relentlessly consumerist, one apparently achieved without conscious irony or awareness. The 'city fathers', in making this choice, seem completely unaware of the critique of modernity set out above and elsewhere. The point is that consumerism has its price: increased materialism by itself results in lower levels of well-being; the consumerist treadmill takes an enormous toll at the community level, resulting in both fewer social ties and less civic engagement; and consumer spending represents an assault on the biosphere. We should, perhaps, expect civic leaders to show a somewhat less uncritical embrace of consumer values in their understandable efforts to promote their city and its future.

CHAPTER FIVE
Why change is inevitable

If, as we have argued up to now, the values of our society are part of the problem, what are the prospects for a reversal? Our analysis is that the values of modernity – materialism, individualism, consumerism, scientism and economism – have a considerable hold on our society and our leaders. Like the frog sitting in water slowly being heated to boiling point, we seem oblivious to the malign effects of this environment. Our values may be shifting a little – not least because of problems such as the global banking crisis, the apparent meltdown of the European currency, and global warming – but probably not enough for us to embark on the level and nature of change that would make a real difference. This is why we believe that continuing deterioration in trends for obesity, alcohol-related harm, well-being and inequality is almost inevitable.

At this point some might point out that current policy in Scotland is dedicated to reducing inequality, combating obesity, improving well-being and promoting sensible drinking. Surely this must count as evidence that our values are egalitarian and pro-health? Whilst that may be true in part, such values struggle in the face of the prevailing ethos and the power of culture outlined above.

Something more substantial than government policy is needed: we suggest that the great ecological and economic challenges of our age represent an opportunity to reframe our current assumptions and ethos. These challenges are, of course, a threat but they may also represent our best opportunity. If change is inevitable, if we are forced to change by larger forces, can we use this to create opportunities for improved health and well-being?

Change is inevitable because it is built into the nature of life. Almost every aspect of life is characterised by growth, peak and decline: this is true of species, physiological systems, businesses and much else. Humanity itself now faces a series of linked external threats, derived from exponential growth in a number of key areas which will lead to certain decline and possible collapse unless we change trajectory rapidly. We know that change is inevitable because exponential growth cannot continue indefinitely in a finite system. We will explore several of these interlinked threats in this chapter but firstly we will examine the idea of 'carrying capacity'.

Arran is one of Scotland's most beautiful islands and on its coast is Lamlash bay, a natural harbour that was used by the Navy during World War II and by pleasure craft today. In the bay is Holy Isle, which is now used by a colony of Buddhists as a retreat. At the entrance to the bay is the much smaller Hamilton Rock. Tourists enjoy the boat trip to view the sights and, while one of us was on such a trip, the skipper of the tourist boat asked if there were any questions. One of the party asked 'at what size does a rock become an island?' The answer is defined by the Inland Revenue, who determine the level of tax to be paid by landowners who include islands in their estates. The tax man has decided that a Scottish island is a piece of land surrounded by sea that is large enough to sustain eight sheep all year round!

This is as simple and straightforward a definition of carrying capacity as we have encountered. Whether an island can sustain eight sheep will depend on the amount of grass and fresh water available and, clearly, there are some islands that are too small (like Hamilton Rock) to meet this definition. The carrying capacity is self-evidently finite and is a function of the physical resources of the island. Yet, this definition is not as straightforward as it might seem. The landowner could sustain sheep on a smaller island either by bringing grass and water to the sheep from another area or by enhancing the island's grass production with fertilizer. The point, of course, is that importing resources is a strategy that can be used to artificially enhance the carrying capacity. By the same logic, if we define carrying capacity as the maximum permanently supportable population, any land area of the globe has a finite carrying capacity for humans and the globe as a whole has a finite carrying capacity. The fact that there is debate over the estimates of global carrying capacity should not blind us to the unequivocal fact that it is finite.

This issue is important at two levels. At a local level, human numbers have frequently exceeded carrying capacity (using the technologies available at the time to extract resources) and this has led to wars. For example, it has been argued that the killing of one ethnic group by another on the scale witnessed in Rwanda was a war of carrying capacity and reflected a growing shortage of agricultural land in that fertile but densely populated country. At a planetary level, several authorities are now arguing that the world's population, with its current technologies and consumption patterns, has already exceeded the planet's carrying capacity.

Although carrying capacity is finite, it is not fixed. Industrialisation made available the accumulated solar energy of many millennia. It increased the proportion of the earth's surface that has been exploited by humans and massively increased our capacity to grow and move food. By drawing on energy stores from the past, industrialisation moved at a fast enough pace to create wealth that led to an increase in human numbers and a rise in per capita wealth. One positive side effect of this process is that some of the most densely populated spots on hearth, like London, New York, Hong Kong or Tokyo, are also among the most prosperous, healthy and well nourished. People in these global centres of wealth creation have in recent years talked about the evolution of a 'weightless economy' that relies on ideas rather than materials to create wealth. Yet, the resource upon which this exponential rise in human numbers and prosperity has been based is finite, drawn from the past, arguably stolen from the future and potentially toxic (in terms of global warming) to the planet.

We also need to face up to the fact that the consumption patterns and technologies that we are employing to maintain our unsustainable lifestyles are changing the habitats on which we depend. There are plenty of examples in nature where organisms have such an impact on their environments that their own survival is undermined. Yeast, for example, is an organism used to brew alcohol. Yeasts that are introduced by the brewer enjoy the resource-rich environment and multiply rapidly. They consume the sugar and multiply but in doing so they change the environment, with the production of carbon dioxide. The consequences are fatal to the yeast. In a parallel example, when autumn rains wash leaves in large numbers into a pond, the spring sunshine and the decaying detritus create the circumstances that allow algae in the pond to bloom. But, as with the yeast, this is not a sustainable ecosystem but one that has been provided with an unrepeatable injection of nutrients. Once that source has been used up, the crash is inevitable.

Fossil fuels are the equivalent of our autumn leaves and decaying detritus. They have created a 'bloom' in human numbers. We have outgrown the carrying capacity of our planet by virtue of a carbon-based economy and have massively exceeded the numbers that can be sustained without the cheap energy provided by oil and other fossil fuels. We face the prospect that further expansion of population will gradually force humanity to divert more and more resources to cope with the problems arising from increasing human numbers and activity. Eventually, so much resource will be diverted to solving these problems that it will become impossible to sustain further growth in industrial output. When industry declines, society can no longer sustain greater and greater output in other economic sectors: food, services and other consumption. When these sectors stop growing, population growth also ceases.

The end of exponential growth in a finite system may take a variety of forms. It could occur as a collapse or an uncontrolled decline. A more desirable future is that the end of such growth occurs as a smooth adaptation of the human footprint to the carrying capacity of the globe. Importantly, it is possible to generate scenarios that plot an orderly end to growth followed by a long period of relatively high human welfare. What is impossible is to imagine that the current growth of economic activity and consumption can continue indefinitely.

The idea of our ecological footprint has been used to illustrate the limits of the planet's carrying capacity. The idea is relatively simple. It compares human demands on nature with the biosphere's ability to regenerate resources and provide services. A calculation is made to find out what acreage of land and sea is needed to fully sustain a given population. The calculation needs to include land for food and other resources as well as land to absorb pollutants produced by that population. In this way it is possible to calculate the footprint of a city, a country or the whole world's population. Incidentally, this work has demonstrated why densely populated cities can be incredibly wealthy. They have a massive footprint and without access through trade to vast tracts of land, they could not survive. Using this approach, a growing literature highlights the conclusion that we have gone beyond the human carrying capacity of the environment by continuing with behaviours that are no longer appropriate for our circumstances.

The carrying capacity of the earth to sustain life in the long term was surpassed by human demands sometime in the 1980s. This assumes that all of the earth's capacity is available for human use. In recent years, it has become more apparent that aspects of the earth's biodiversity create resilience and stability to various ecosystems. Some argue that it is prudent, since these processes are not well understood, to leave a significant buffer as an 'insurance policy'. Using the Brundtland Commission suggestion of 12%, then it appears that humans over-ran the carrying capacity of the earth in the early 1970s: by the end of the millennium the extent of the overshoot was 40%. These data say nothing about the rate at which resources are being depleted and so cannot suggest how long remaining biosphere resources will be able to continue in this way. Global average per capita demand by the end of the twentieth century equated to about 2.3 hectares. In the US the average was 9.7 hectares per person and the UK 4.7 hectares per person. Such data have been used to calculate that Americans need five earth-like planets, and Europeans need three such planets, to maintain current lifestyles. Clearly, only 'one planet living' is truly sustainable.

We in Europe kick-started the modern age of abundance by taking advantage of resources from other lands: not just the Americas but also Australasia and parts of Asia and Africa. We sustained our largest period of growth by drawing down natural resources accumulated over vast periods of time, thus denying them to future populations. There are no 'new worlds' for us to further exploit and a variety of finite resources will peak in their production very soon if they have not done so already. This is the true nature of our circumstances.

Growth in human numbers is a key factor in this story but one with a surprising and currently poorly understood ending. The good news is that the 'population time bomb' has been defused and, if we act wisely, other threats could be too. Writers in the 1960s, like Paul Erlich, predicted a population time bomb that would lead to a global population in excess of 20 billion resulting, he predicted, in famine, war and disease. His projections were based on the extrapolation of population growth trends of his day. Instead, we now preside over a challenging but potentially manageable scenario in which the global population will peak during the twenty-first century at less than half of Erlich's estimate. This should be a warning that the future cannot be predicted – but it should also encourage us to think that global threats can be managed if we respond appropriately.

The reason we are experiencing a more benign outcome than was predicted is that much of the world has moved, more rapidly than we once imagined, through what is called the demographic transition. In a pre-industrial society, although birth rates are very high, they are balanced by death rates. The result is very slow population growth. As the transition begins, small improvements in prosperity and technology create an imbalance between death rates and birth rates. Britain entered this stage of transition in the late eighteenth century, and countries in this stage today include Yemen, Afghanistan, Palestine and much of Sub-Saharan Africa. Death rates decrease rapidly because of improvements in food supply, better sanitation, improved water supply, effective sewerage systems, growing scientific knowledge, improved education and improvement of basic health care. However, birth rates tend not to decrease in this stage of the transition as culture still remains largely the same. The resulting imbalance creates a large and rapid increase in population. This growth is solely due to the decrease in death rates and is not due to an increase in fertility.

In the next stage the population moves towards stability. This is driven by rising prosperity and an accompanying change in culture: death rates continue to fall but birth rates fall even faster. There are many reasons why the birth rates fall: the population gains access to contraception; wages increase; urbanisation proceeds; better education is provided (particularly for girls); and a society becomes less dependent on children as an economic resource. This is the process through which much of the world has already passed.

During the twentieth century the global population did mushroom and continues to grow, but towards the end of the century the rate of growth declined. During the 1970s women around the world had nearly six children on average: now that figure has declined to 2.45 and in some countries it is as low as 1. Current predictions are that the globe's population will peak at about 9.5 billion in 2070 and then slowly decline. Replacement levels of fertility are 2.1 per couple, yet, in Italy it has fallen to 1.3 and the general trend in Europe is for lowering fertility rates, although not all have gone as far as Italy. Japan has very similar rates and in Asia as a whole the fertility rate is down from 2.4 in 1970 to 1.5 today. China's rate is down from 6.06 to 1.8 and declining. The poorest Asian countries still have high fertility (Afghanistan is 7.1). Importantly, East Asia has plummeted rapidly to low levels of fertility it took Europe years to attain. It has, for instance, taken 115 years (1865–1980) for the proportion of older people in France to increase from 7% to 14%. The equivalent time for the same doubling to happen in China is expected to be 27 years (2000–27).

One consequence of low fertility rates is rapid population

ageing. Yet, while populations are declining and ageing across the more affluent parts, there is still rapid population growth in many other parts of the world. Birth rates are high in much of Africa: populations in countries like Uganda, Burkina Faso and Congo will treble or more by 2050. Both extremes are associated with different challenges. If Europe continues with a fertility rate of 1.5, the population will drop by half in 65 years. If Africa continues with rapid growth, it will need to achieve massive expansions in employment and infrastructure. The conventional wisdom about demographic transition is that when people are poor they have many children. After all, if half your children die before adulthood then you need to have enough to ensure that there is someone to look after you in old age. But when you get richer, family size starts dropping. The health of your children improves; girls go to school and get jobs, marry later and have children later. However, there are exceptions to this generalised pattern. Korea was not rich when fertility declined. The Gulf States are rich but have high fertility. In short, cultural and other factors are also important. The world's highest fertility rates are to be found in the most religious countries. The exception to this is the very low fertility rates in Catholic southern Europe.

Scotland now has an ageing population and the change in age structure has very significant implications for the future of Scotland's economy, for family life, and for the planning and delivery of services. In 2004, 35% of the adult population was aged over 50, and 7% over 75 years. By 2024 those percentages are projected to be 44% and 11%. To put it another way, there will be 2.2 million people aged 50 years or over and more than half a million aged 75 or over.

Alongside this, there will be fewer people in the traditional working-age group. The average age of people in the workforce will be higher due to both population change and the impact of UK policy to extend working lives. The impact is much greater in some parts of Scotland than in others. Dumfries and Galloway, for example, has a projected fall of over 40 % in the 30 to 44 age group over the period 2002 to 2017.

The challenge of responding to an ageing population is no longer confined to industrialised countries: currently, of the 11 largest elderly populations in the world, eight come from within the developing world (China, India, Brazil, Indonesia, Pakistan, Mexico, Bangladesh and Nigeria). With few exceptions, the elderly are now the fastest growing segment in the developing world. The ageing of society has implications for the old-age dependency ratio – the ratio of individuals aged 65 and over in the population to the size of the economically active segment of the population. The conventional wisdom is that this shift in balance will damage the economy and create serious problems for health and social care services: not only will there be an insufficient number of tax payers to pay for the costs of the NHS, but there will not be sufficient numbers of young people to work as health and social care professionals. However, these predictions depend entirely on the health and vitality of the whole population as it ages.

As we age the risk of disease and death increases. The reason for this is that ageing leads to a progressive, generalised impairment of function resulting in a loss of adaptive response. Two factors influence this risk: the rate of physiological decline and the risk of external assaults from the environment. A wide range of physiological functions decline with age: examples include the efficiency of lung function, circulation, muscles and nerves. There would seem to be a genetic element to this process of decline but it is also influenced by factors like environment, lifestyle and nutrition. Under certain influences this decline can accelerate but attention to behaviour and environment can significantly slow the decline. For example, those who do not use their large muscle groups will lose strength. Sometimes the level of decline is such that we define it as pathological. For example, an individual who smokes and eats a poor diet may experience changes that reduce coronary blood flow and lead to ischaemic heart disease. The key point is that there is a slow decline in a wide range of physiological functions with age but that the *rate* of decline is amenable to a large variety of environmental and behavioural interventions. One of the keys to healthy ageing is the manipulation of behaviour and environment to slow the rate of physiological decline as much as possible.

External assaults include accidents, trauma, infections and any factor that threatens our physiological function sufficiently to cause disease or death. Obviously, the environment in which we live influences the frequency and scale of external assaults. Also, our ability to withstand infection or trauma depends on the reserve capacity of our physiological systems. For example, pneumonia in a young healthy person with lungs that have a large reserve capacity is much less likely to be fatal than the same infection in an older person who has a lifelong history of smoking. The conclusion to be drawn from this analysis is that the key to healthy ageing is to ensure that physiological decline is kept to a minimum and occurs in parallel across the major body systems, while external assaults like trauma and infection are kept to a minimum.

The term 'compression of morbidity' is used to describe an optimistic scenario where increasing proportions of the population will achieve these twin aims and live long, healthy lives in which death will be preceded by a very short period of ill health (morbidity). An alternative theory is that we will see an extension to the period of ill health and poor functioning at the end of life, that is, an extension of morbidity. Two mechanisms will drive this. First, the age of onset of poor function or disease will remain unchanged as influences like smoking and diet give rise to, for example, coronary heart disease or obstructive airways disease during mid life. At the same time, medical and environmental interventions will allow people to survive to an older age. The consequence will be increased longevity but with an extended period of morbidity or ill health during older age.

We have spent some time on these themes because they are an antidote to fatalistic depression and inaction. The world heeded the potential impact of rising population numbers, learned from the countries that had already experienced the demographic transition, and applied the lessons to good effect elsewhere. The size of the peak in the global population will depend on whether we can bring prosperity to the parts of the world that remain poor and are still trapped in continuing exponential increases in population. The new but inevitable challenge is population ageing, but the choice between compression and extension of morbidity in populations that are ageing depends on our ability and willingness to change our behaviours and environments.

Another question is that of how we feed the world's current population of nearly seven billion people, far less the projected number. This is not easily answered. Taken together, hunger and malnutrition account for about 53% of preschool deaths in the world: each year they kill 6 million children, one every five seconds. It is tempting to suggest that the solution to this problem is to grow more food. However, we need to remember that we live in a world where, remarkably, there are now more obese people than malnourished or hungry people. This suggests that the overall volume of food supply is not the only or perhaps even the main problem. Most of the 'grow more' solutions are also affected by the impacts of other challenges that we now face. For example, chemical fertilisers, the backbone of the 'green revolution' since the 1960s, are intimately linked to the price of oil – the 'green' revolution was in fact 'black'. Also, valuable agricultural land, which could be used for food, is being passed over to the growing of biofuel. What is the likely impact on Scotland? The price of food is likely to rise. After World War II, the average Scottish family spent nearly 40% of the household budget on food. Today it is less than 10% but we should anticipate rising prices over the next few decades. We will need to think seriously about food security, food miles and our current wastage of food.

Globally, deforestation and loss of mature forest has been accelerated more recently by demand for timber and the clearing of rainforest for commercial crops. From about the mid-1800s, the planet has experienced an unprecedented rate of change and destruction of forests worldwide: it is in the world's great tropical rainforests where the destruction is most pronounced at the current time and where wholesale felling is having an adverse effect on biodiversity. Unless significant measures are taken on a worldwide basis to preserve them, by 2030 there will only be 10% remaining with another 10% in a degraded condition. Deforestation affects the amount of water in the soil and groundwater and the moisture in the atmosphere. Forests also help to retain topsoil intact and support considerable biodiversity, providing valuable habitats for wildlife. Moreover, forests foster medicinal conservation with forest biotopes being a major, irreplaceable source of new drugs. Deforestation can destroy genetic variations, such as crop resistance, irretrievably.

There is now strong evidence that the earth is warming and that this trend is being accelerated by human activity. Humans are now pouring large amounts of CO_2 and other greenhouse gases into the atmosphere. Data from ice cores show that levels of CO_2, methane and nitrous oxide have risen significantly above normal interglacial levels. As these gases are part of the earth's thermostat, such increases are a cause for great concern. Data from the last hundred years show significant rises in temperature on all continents. Satellite data from the last thirty years show significant increases in mean surface temperature, particularly in northern latitudes. One can see the impacts of these changes in retreating glaciers, ice cover and melting permafrost. One effect of the current retreat will be the release of further methane trapped in the ice, thereby accelerating global warming. Forecasting the effects of greenhouse gases is far from perfect, and is largely done through the development of computer simulations. While these have limitations, such models suggest that there has been clear human forcing of warming, over and above that of natural processes. This pattern looks set to continue and we can see that, despite all claimed effort, the rate of CO_2 emissions has doubled since 2000. Empirical data from 2003 onwards suggest that the initial scenarios of the International Panel of Climate Change are being outstripped. We are most likely past the point of being able to avoid warming altogether.

Two further exponential growth curves are also important to this context – energy use and money. Energy use is currently going though an exponential growth phase and, because there is a finite amount of fossil fuel energy, cannot keep growing indefinitely. Much development over the last 100 years has been based on the availability of cheap energy. This includes the production of fertilisers which support intensive farming techniques; the 'just-in-time' retail trade supported by a massive truck fleet; and the out-of-town shopping centres and suburbia developed without need for public transport. Almost every aspect of the society in which we live is currently dependent either directly or indirectly on the availability of cheap energy. For energy, the problem comes when the peak in production (of oil, gas, uranium or whatever) occurs because the second half of the resource is more difficult (and thus more expensive in terms of money and energy) to extract. As energy has become more expensive, energy companies will exploit alternative sources (like oil from shale deposits). This may delay the peak in oil production but it takes more energy to extract oil from these sources, so the cost will remain high.

As for money, we are not economists so will have to be cautious in what we say. Nevertheless, it is a matter of fact that money is created by debt, that a continuing growth of money is built into the current system and, in the years leading up to the crash of 2008, we saw an exponential growth in credit. As long as the supply of credit keeps growing, loans and interest can be paid off. But, if there is a major default or the money supply stops, the whole system collapses. It is to prevent this type of collapse that governments are buying up bad debts. Scotland, as part of the UK, is one of the most indebted countries in the world. The UK borrowed more in the seven years preceding the 2008 crash than in all of its previous history. We need to repay personal debt, official government debt and a whole series of unfunded liabilities like Private Finance Initiative hospitals and schools.

The economy in Scotland currently relies heavily on financial services, retail, tourism and the public sector (health, education etc.). A world financial crisis precipitated by any one or a combination of the factors outlined above would almost certainly damage our economy and create a major threat to our health and well-being. At that point, change would be inevitable but extremely difficult. The challenge of leadership is to change before it is – painfully – forced upon us.

'. . . we are currently living through a "change of age" which is simultaneously challenging, unsettling and inevitable.'

CHAPTER SIX
Who is showing the way?

'Every few hundred years in Western history there occurs a sharp transformation. Within a few short decades, society – its worldview, its basic values, its social and political structures, its arts, its key institutions – rearranges itself. . . We are currently living through such a time.' Peter Drucker

We have written this book because we believe we are currently living through a 'change of age' which is simultaneously challenging, unsettling and inevitable. Earlier chapters have discussed the role of poor health and the challenges of ecological and economic breakdown to Scotland's future. Many people seem to realise this, at a deep intuitive level, but feel helpless to respond. Our political leaders tend to respond with short term 'fixes' while our experts work in specialist silos. Something new and different is needed. Scotland has successfully negotiated a change of age before. When we moved from an agricultural to an industrial economy, progress happened through the efforts of a resilient and inventive people in a difficult and challenging context. We need to look for such efforts in our own contemporary Scotland, nourish them and learn from them. Our conventional metaphors of fixing and building, predicting and planning will no longer suffice.

Our current change of age also provides an opportunity to reframe the current assumptions and ethos of modern societies. Experience suggests that we will probably make only small voluntary changes for health and well-being benefits. However, if change is inevitable, if we are forced to change by larger forces, then we can use this opportunity to reframe some of the debates that inform public health policy. If the future is emergent then, by definition, there will be no blueprint. We cannot look to science or technology or government or ideology or any one thing on its own to provide a solution.

During a series of 'learning journeys' across Scotland, as part of our research fieldwork, we held many fascinating conversations with diverse people and organisations. As a result we can report that new ways of thinking, being and doing are now emerging: we have seen examples of transformational change. We were inspired, for example, by what we learned from the International Futures Forum, the Glasgow Centre for Integrative Care, Govan Together, the Galgael Trust, the Falkland Centre for Stewardship, the Geopoetics Society on the island of Luing, the Fife Diet Project, emerging social enterprises, diverse family businesses and much more. These are remarkably diverse examples with some fundamental elements in common.

Another book in this series by Alf and Ewan Young, *The New Road: Charting Scotland's inspirational communities* – describes a similar range of inspiring examples in Scotland.

Here, we will focus on just two: David Reilly, creator of the Wellness Enhancement Learning (WEL) programme, and Andrew Lyon, who works with International Futures Forum (IFF). By so doing, we can explore elements of the new integrated inner and outer worlds that may need to emerge. Whilst we present these two examples in part because of the depth of collaboration the AfterNow project has enjoyed with both, there is no sense in which we are promoting them as 'the answer'. Rather, we aim to share how their ways of thinking, being and doing may help others navigate the future.

The Wellness Enhancement Learning (WEL) project was originally developed by David Reilly, working in collaboration with patients living with chronic illness. The programme was subsequently extended to other groups of patients and NHS staff. We were struck by the way participants from all groups talked about the nature of the change they experienced – a 'healing shift' which leads towards greater self-care and self-compassion *and* a greater sense of empowering responsibility. We suggest that greater understanding of this phenomenon is required, given that such change appears within the capability of all of us. David Reilly has been a core member of the AfterNow team of collaborators, and the two projects (AfterNow and WEL) have run in tandem since early 2006. Whilst AfterNow explored the impact of external (but internalised) cultural shifts on our well-being, WEL explored (and put into practice) the human potential for self-healing, resilience and well-being.

David is a consultant physician who is currently the Scottish Government's National Clinical Lead for Integrative Care. He graduated in medicine and pursued a rigorous conventional training in Adult Medicine and General Practice. However, he judged the 'treatment factory' mindset that junior doctors encounter failed, in many cases, to meet many of the complex needs of patients and even tended to brutalise staff. At this point he considered giving up medicine altogether, but then concluded that he had to find a different way of being a doctor. He began by seeking to learn from his own patients and developed a distinctive approach to healing, innovation and change. At the core of it lies a shift in the practitioner – away from engagement shaped by the questionable old map of – 'What can we do to fix you/ your situation?' – to a map that asks 'What can we do to help you release your own self-sustaining capacity?' The aim is to be 'integrative' – reducing fragmentation and increasing coherence within the person and their care. He led the creation of the NHS Centre for Integrative Care, which was formerly the Glasgow Homeo-pathic Hospital. As part of this he led the creation of a new building to house the Centre guided by a desire for this hospital to be a house of healing rather than a treatment factory. It cost the same per square metre to build as any other NHS facility, but it is very different in appearance and effect. It has curved corridors, glass walls overlooking a garden for each inpatient room, and furnishings and artworks that speak to the aesthetic side of our natures.

This hospital is part of the National Health Service and patients are referred by GPs and hospital consultants. These patients have usually exhausted all the usual lines of investigation, diagnosis and treatment and are often referred as a last option. The design of the hospital, with its emphasis on natural daylight, art displays and gardens is integral to the process of healing. David told us about one young patient who had said how sad it was that the flowers all died in autumn; she had not known that they would return in spring. Her life had been so far removed from natural processes that winter, for her, meant death and endings. Yet, we can also think of illness as a time of 'winter' in life; from that metaphorical 'death' we can, if all goes well, return. And on that return we can often re-perceive the world, in the light of that experience. David went on to explain that the purpose of art in a hospital setting is to reflect the idea that healing itself is a creative process, with the life force as the medium. Inherent in this notion is the idea that underneath our suffering and illness as human beings, we are fundamentally whole. Healing is the re-discovery of that wholeness.

David's contention is that it is possible to use the encounter between doctor and patient to create a powerful consultation that promotes a healing response. This response is derived from the positive power of two humans focused on a shared challenge. He often works with patients who have spent a great deal of time in the National Health Service system with little or no improvement. For many, the NHS approach, one seeking to discover what has gone wrong with the human machine and then put it right, does not work. Instead, he works with each patient to discover the inherent, if latent, strength and inner healing capacity of that individual. David explores a 'germinative' approach, one based in understanding that individual human encounters can affect the mind-body continuum. His approach neither devalues the technical skill of the physician nor the sciences which underpin this, but he sees the encounter as being about more than techniques and tools, useful though these may be in some cases. In this way he is seeking to transcend but also include all that is good in modern medicine. The results are often transformative.

He studies examples of successful transformations and works backwards ('reverse engineers') to an understanding of the germinative conditions and creative processes. In this way therapeutic encounters call upon creativity, learning, multiple inputs from many disciplines, scientific learning, art, and respect for 'the other' in the process. It works for the patient because it validates their humanity and brings them into the process as an active participant, not simply a bundle of symptoms, problems or objectified characteristics – a damaged or broken machine. It reduces their medical dependence, enabling their own strength. It works for the physician because it yields better results: satisfying and effective patient contact decreases the chance of 'burn-out'. It therefore enriches the experience of both partners in the encounter and fosters an active mind-body link in both doctor and patient.

The main ingredients of these positive encounters are, clearly, human! Whilst the model appears strongly directional, implicit within it is the learning and development that emerges from each encounter to influence subsequent practice. From the complexity, we would highlight here three of the key components at work in catalyzing the healing response. These might be coded as: 'presence'; 'the dance'; and 'mobilizing inner resources'. A brief summary of these components is given here:

Presence: The physician must become deeply present, mindful, there as a whole person, not simply a collection of skills learned during medical training. 'The consultation begins before the consultation' – with the practitioner learning to increase presence by practice, and then preparing themselves before and during each encounter. This 'self-activation' deepens active sensing – the process of tuning in and listening to what is going on, and a natural silent alertness to cues and non-verbal communications – like really listening to or playing music, we take in the whole complexity, with sensitivity to the active context which the person brings to the encounter – sharpened by awareness that their well-being is at stake. Any chance of a meaningful consultation could be over in the first few seconds, as it only takes that long for a person to sense a lack of interest or distraction. With this awareness as background, and a genuine attention to welcome and conditions that will support the meeting, the meeting begins. Gradually, the space that opens is one of deepening empathy, connected relationship, and compassion – the healing space.

'The dance': This is a metaphor for the interaction that then takes place between the partners after the encounter space has been successfully created, and a 'join-up' has been created of safe relationship. Active listening, sensitivity, and an ability to engage are crucial to the success of the process. The dialogue – which may include silence, reflection, and the use of image and metaphor – brings the active and blocking inner maps to light (the *habitus*) and explores their effects. The need for change and, through emergent creative process and skill, a journey of inspiring change is initiated, motivation ignited, as the person is helped to examine their own predicament, ways of approaching it, reasons and needs for change, and fresh approaches. Accessing a compassion-based, self-care relationship has emerged as a particularly important focus here. This sounds solemn, and sometimes is, but often is disarmingly light, and full of humour.

Mobilising inner resources: If 'presence' can be manifested and 'the dance' goes well, the inner perceptions shift, the resources of the person are mobilised and these become available to the subsequent healing or change processes over time. The participants become allies in a joint venture, each playing their part as creative healers, rather than subject and object over a prescription pad. Overarching it all is the vision of the strength latent in the person, and the core purpose of the work – releasing capacity and improving self-care in the service of reducing suffering and distress, and enhancing well-being.

We suggest that these three ingredients will be needed in many other settings (education, social work, business and so on) if we are to move beyond the technical and reductionist mindsets that so characterise modernity. For example, a housing co-op may provide a service for five hundred people; a secondary school may be responsible for fifteen hundred young people; a hospital for a catchment area might cover several hundred thousand people; a local authority has responsibility for a wide range of services; a business corporation may cross international boundaries. Are there principles and guidelines, approaches and actions that operate well across different scales of human activity, which resonate with the WEL approach? We believe there may be. Our proposition is that mobilising the energy within ourselves and others will provide a basis for positive change. This is set against the system of modernist institutions that currently prevail. These have yielded a great deal over the years in terms of improvement and care. Yet their size and culture tends to douse the commitment and energy of those who join them in order to do good.

In a bid to 'upscale' the insights gained from one-to-one consultations, a group-based WEL programme was created in Glasgow and is now extending its work as The PrimaryWEL version in the community of Nairn, in the North East of Scotland. We visited this new arm of the programme as part of the third phase of the AfterNow work, 'in search of transformational change'. Over the course of three days, one of the GPs in the Nairn Healthcare Group and co-director of the WEL in Nairn, enabled us to meet and speak to a range of practice staff. Many of these had participated in the StaffWEL version of the programme which was run before the patient version to see if a supportive cultural shift could be seeded. We were also able to speak to a number of people who had taken part in the programme. We have to acknowledge that we are grappling with fragments in trying to convey the complexity of embodied knowledge and experience through the limited tool of language. What we observed, however, was that the success of the programme pivoted on the concept of compassion, 'presence' (i.e. participants bringing their full selves to the sessions), and the competence and authenticity of the facilitator.

We asked participants to outline their understanding of what the WEL programme was about, to describe any impact it had, and to identify the crux of change. We summarise below the main theme which emerged during discussions, which seems to best capture and reflect the experiences and perceptions of WEL participants, staff and patients. That theme centres on participants' efforts to describe the process of self-change stimulated by the programme, and their understanding of the outcomes of that process. This experience can perhaps best be expressed (albeit imprecisely) as a 'healing journey' – one which took place in the context of a change in mindset and worldview. Beneath this overarching theme, the stories we were told possessed a number of noticeable elements: recognition of how and why certain forms of illness develop; acceptance of and responsibility for self-care; and enhanced capacity for self-compassion. Other changes remarked on by participants included: improved family relationships as a result of greater patience and gentleness; learning which aspects of the programme best suited them; greater individual confidence in their own ability to change for the better.

The WEL programme in Nairn has been established by the joint efforts of Drs David Reilly and Audrey Banks, with the support of many other staff working in general practice and primary care in Nairn, and a network of partners. This does not mean that its success here may be unique to Nairn, given its longevity in Glasgow. Nevertheless, it seemed to us that the GP partnership in particular provided the thoughtful, supporting, enquiring and caring context which allowed Audrey and David the scope and space needed to develop the means for the 'shift' in experience and mindset which we witnessed in patients and staff over the course of three days. This development derived in turn from Audrey's initial training with David, informed by David's practice over many decades. The sense we were left with was that of a Practice genuinely keen to explore the nature of their relationships with patients and community, in the hope of playing a key role in a different form of care process, one with the potential to lead to greater resilience and well-being for some of their patients, their families and their community. Conventional NHS practice, we were told, can sometimes – unintentionally – stifle, even crush, the deep impulse to care for others that most practitioners would want to bring to their daily work. Many health care providers also acknowledge the limits of the current system when dealing with some forms of chronic illness. Anything which might truly help such patients was welcomed. More broadly, we also picked up the sense that Nairn itself might be an encouraging place in which to site this endeavour – one where a sense of community still exists and provided a space for something new to grow.

We heard that the WEL programme is a series of four weekly discussion/teaching sessions, led by David Reilly, in which patient participants reflect about their illness, about what was happening to them, and why. New areas of learning are introduced each week. Participants told us that they found they '*took a good hard look*' at themselves, right from the very beginning of the programme. They brought varied expectations to the course: some were '*determined not to be put down*' by their condition; one spoke of the programme '*raising awareness but lowering [unrealistic] expectations*'. Others, before undertaking the programme, had '*wanted their life back*' – to be as they were before. This understanding had shifted over time: '*WEL is not about a cure*', said one participant, '*it's about how to live better with whatever life throws at you*'. For one, this was almost a process of rebirth: '*I realised the old me had to die to let a new me come through*'.

For some, particularly staff participants, the knowledge

provided was not always new but had never been fully internalised or practised. For others, the process of learning was '*enlightening*', even '*astounding*'. More significantly, it provided all participants with the conviction that there was something they could do – actions they could take – to improve their relationship with and care for the self, relationships with others, and with the world of work. The ready acceptance of personal responsibility for self-healing was very striking: the programme apparently generated neither resistance nor anger in participants. In part, this was attributed to David Reilly giving them '*permission*' to freely make their own choices ('*I'm not your Dad – you have to take care of yourself*'), but also because they sensed that he cared about their well-being. Participants spoke about a gradual realisation of what they were learning, and being able to take information home and dip into this at times of need. The information itself was valued, but one judged that '*it's not just what the programme does – it's how it does it*'. This 'how' involved giving people time to truly focus on themselves – '*sweeping away the pretences, the stories, the unhelpful maps*'. They were enabled to tell their stories without this becoming a process of self-indulgence, one participant told us, although neither was it a simple thing. '*I had to face myself and accept myself*', said one. '*That's a huge thing*'.

In response to the programme, participants spoke of a '*change of world view*', a '*change of identity*'. '*It was about changing who I am, not just how I think*', said one: '*a mindshift I can't describe or put my finger on*', said another, '*but it feels permanent*'. This '*changed mindset*' remained, even when patients struggled with their new forms of practice and '*fell off the wagon*'. They had also learned the '*simple message of accepting that there are some things you can't control'* – difficult learning in itself, when cherishing the initial belief that *'I should function the way I used to before I was ill'*. Time and again people told us that they were encouraged and enabled to develop a sense of self-love or self-compassion, to put their own needs first when necessary. For many of the women present this was clearly a novel idea, as the needs and demands of other people had formerly governed life. At its most basic, they understood the need to *'take care of yourself, as no-one else will'*. Many used the metaphor of the self as a plant, introduced during the programme, and clearly understood that they had often neglected that plant in the past.

'The biggest thing I've learned,' said one participant, *'is to say no'* in a context where *'I needed to do everything for everyone.'*

'It's about being honest with myself,' said another, *'knowing I'd led myself down this path.'*

'We're responsible for ourselves.' said yet another.

Some described their learning as becoming *'engrained yet effortless'*, and *'waking up to things we've always known'*. Many spoke about developing a new *'gentleness'*, to self and others. Some acknowledged that they had long had a difficult relationship with food, and that nutrition was an area of struggle for them. But eating well was understood as just one component of a broader change involved in living well. So, for some, their diet had not changed greatly, compared to the new way they thought about themselves. The point of change in mindset and worldview could, however, only be expressed in fragmentary ways: '*something clicks*' was the phrase used by some, as the closest they could get to articulating this complex phenomenon. It seems likely that the *healing shift* spoken about cannot be captured in words as its experience is embodied and half-conscious, rather than fully cognitive.

Another sub-theme, remarked on by patients and staff alike, was the benefit of both groups participating in the relevant programme. Shared knowledge and experience enabled a new vocabulary between these groups and a new relationship. '*Ten years ago,*' said one, '*you'd never have thought your GP would be training with you.*' It gave patients a sense of value that their doctors and other health care providers were willing to join them in the learning process. Staff understood that WEL was 'not about creating a dependency of patients', whereas patients said 'we need to think for ourselves, and we need to see it's not their job to do everything – that's not sustainable'. Staff commented that 'preventive medicine' is not necessarily exciting or stimulating, whereas 'encouraging flourishing and well-being is'.

The changes and benefits noted were not confined solely to participants' individual experiences. A surprising number – staff and patients – told us that their families had noticed and benefited from changes; for many, this meant less conflict, fewer arguments, and more harmonious family relationships. Changes in the way the family functioned were also noticed. One participant with teenage daughters told us that her home environment had completely changed and that the '*calmness in the house is incredible*'. Others, too, spoke of a new capacity to '*take a deep breath and step back*', rather than reacting with anger which benefited no-one, least of all themselves. *'The kids used to say I never listened to them. Everything was a rush, all timed. It's not like that anymore.'* Some spoke of changes in wider relationships: *'I learned to listen to other people rather than butting in and taking over conversations.'* Staff spoke of having a greater recognition of other people's circumstances and realising that people don't always understand what affects their lives. For some, this translated into giving their patients far more time – at least an hour, said one nurse, for patients with long-term conditions.

The above can only give a brief and inevitably over-simplified sense of participants' experience of the programme, expressed here in terms of their own learning journey towards greater self-acceptance, responsibility, compassion and personal growth. However, it should also be noted that underpinning participants' efforts to put their experience into words lay a study of more objective measurements of their health status, obtained through blood samples (for example tracking their declined use of processed foods to see if it affects their levels of fasting insulin and Omega 3). Participants mostly welcomed such 'testing' of programme effects as the changes observed over time were powerful: they themselves were the embodied proof of positive change.

By the time around a quarter of the 240 participants in the Nairn Centre had completed the StaffWEL, subsequent staff recruits to the programme were saying they had already begun changes in self-care before they entered the programme, influenced by observation of and discussion with the previous participants. For example, the type of food staff members were eating in the dining room had changed as had the way people were handling work stress. This was evident in the objective measures taken at the point of entry compared to three months before they started the course. A cultural shift seems to be occurring among the staff.

Many participants spontaneously remarked on the potential significance of the WEL programme for other public sector organisations, particularly education and the wider health service. Most were eager to see the programme expand beyond the local health centre and out into the community. This prompted various reflections about the ease of 'transferability' of such a programme: some understood that 'bureaucratisation' and '*rolling it out*' might only succeed in destroying the very spirit of nurturance and growth that made it so effective. The point was also made that a 'teaching manual' would be totally inadequate, in the absence of the experience and practice required, and the 'natural' teaching abilities displayed by David Reilly (who emphasises that he is simply using skills and a practice which have been developed over years but which can be transferable). Notwithstanding such concerns and reservations, there appeared to be a deeply-held enthusiasm amongst participants – staff and patients – for extending the programme to the broader community. They believed that there are many 'growth points' in Nairn that made it a suitable candidate for careful extension. A Civic Conversation is now planned to extend the issues raised by the WEL and Afternow work into the wider community. This will be facilitated by Andrew Lyon of the International Futures Forum (IFF).

International Futures Forum (IFF) was established under

the Direction of Graham Leicester in 2001 to address the 'conceptual emergency' which they perceived to be a consequence of living in the modern world. Graham talks about this crisis as being like the familiar tale of the blind men who, if they could only see the whole, would have recognised the elephant but instead extrapolated from the small part they could feel – the result was that each reached false conclusions. We experience the same 'blindness' as we confront a world of boundless complexity, rapid change and radical interconnectedness. As a consequence there is little chance that any one individual will ever know more than one small piece of the elephant. Furthermore, there are now so many different pieces, which change so rapidly and are all so intimately related one to another, that even if we had the technology to put them all together we would still not be able to make sense of the whole. This raises fundamental questions about our competence in key areas of governance, economy, sustainability and consciousness. IFF argues:

> we are struggling in our work and private lives to meet the demands it is placing on traditional models of organisation, understanding and action. The anchors of identity, morality, cultural coherence and social stability are unravelling and we are losing our bearings. This is a conceptual emergency.

The mission of IFF is to 'restore practical hope and provoke wise initiatives in challenging circumstances' and to 'address complex, messy, seemingly intractable issues – local, global and all levels in between'. The network of individuals involved in IFF works with governments, communities, businesses, foundations and others to support people experiencing a combination of aspiration for something better and frustration that little they do seems to get them nearer their goal. Their aim is to help develop the capacity for transformative innovation rather than simply propping up the old system.

The Afternow project has enjoyed fruitful engagement with several of the people who are central to the work of IFF (in particular, Margaret Hannah, who has been a member of the AfterNow collaboration and Maureen O'Hara and Tony Hodgson who have engaged with us on learning journeys). Dr Margaret Hannah has contributed importantly across the full range of issues addressed by the Afternow project and has made her own distinctive developments more widely in the area of health, well-being and public health. However, our closest and longest collaboration has been with Andrew Lyon and we turn now to his work as an illustration of the inner and outer changes that may be needed in our current context.

Andrew began his career in anthropology, deriving insights and contributing to writing from rural India. Returning to Scotland he moved into public health and made an enormous contribution by leading the Glasgow Healthy Cities project. By the year 2000, he was working on sustainability issues with Forward Scotland and was building extensive and diverse networks while experimenting with fresh ways of working with communities. Andrew considers it a privilege to have worked on these important projects and is proud of much that was achieved. However, he observed that outcomes always turned out to be less than what was hoped for and he began to ask profound questions about why that should be.

This kind of narrative emerged as a recurring theme of our learning journeys. Those who were engaging in transformational change almost all described the discomfiting experience of their deepest values being in conflict with their previous circumstances. This dynamic moved them out of their comfort zone. Each personal account was particular but the common factor was that each wanted to find a way in which they could bring their whole selves to work – to make an authentic contribution.

When we asked Andrew about the roots of the values that had formed his perspective he recounted a formative episode from his youth. 'I was about nine or ten – I was going to the Boys Brigade on a Sunday morning and my father would take me. We were driving down this hill past the Infirmary and my Dad stops the car and says 'I'll be back in a minute son'. So he jumps out the car and he runs up to this woman who's limping down the pavement, and then the next thing he picks her up in his arms and carries her into the Infirmary, and he's away for a few minutes and then he comes back. So I said 'what happened?' He said 'well, I saw that woman limping down the road outside the Infirmary and I thought she must be going there and she was having trouble walking, so I thought I would just go see if I could help her'. I said 'well, I could see that was happening but why did you do that?' He switched off the car engine and he said 'well, see these relationships son, they're the only thing we've got, we don't have anything else, so we need to take care of them'. He started up the car and drove on. That's really stuck with me.' Andrew makes the point that his father was not a learned man: this wasn't something that he had learned from books. He just searched in himself and he said, 'well, this is what I feel'.

In 2001 Andrew became one of the founder members of International Futures Forum (IFF). His role in IFF is the 'converger'. What does he converge? The answer is a set of values, ideas, models, tools and experiences with the 'on the ground' circumstances of people living and working in Scotland.

For example, Andrew brought to the Afternow project ideas from an IFF member based in California – psychologist Maureen O'Hara. Maureen describes three different responses to the types of problems that have been set out so far in this book. The first is *neurotic* and is arguably the most common. This manifests itself as denial coupled with a desire to over-simplify issues and keep the boundaries of information tightly controlled. We encountered examples of this approach wherever we went in Scotland on our learning journeys. One clear manifestation was people clinging to policies and programmes which were in practice simply ineffective or, sometimes, making the problem worse. Andrew's approach is always to 'stand with' people who find themselves in this predicament. There is no sense of criticism because we all feel this response in ourselves.

The second response – which is called *psychotic* – emerges when people's ability to cling to the status quo and the familiar is pushed to the limits. Anger and depression result: anger is directed towards the perceived cause of the anxiety or just more generally (e.g. road rage). Unfortunately, anger and depression erode people's capacity to respond creatively and compassionately to our collective predicament. Another manifestation of this response might be called 'bucolic psychosis': eat, drink and be merry. Again, one does not have to look too hard to find examples in Scotland.

The third response is *transformational*. This occurs when people neither deny the challenge nor tune out, and instead draw on their internal resources to develop new capabilities to grow through new circumstance and thus increase their resilience (at both individual and community levels). Note that the complexity and challenge are not diminished: rather, the capacity to respond is enhanced. In a very real sense, this book is simply an exploration of how people in Scotland might help themselves and each other achieve this transformational response. Encouragingly, the capacity for transformational change seems to be intrinsic to our humanity – we are all capable of this response.

Andrew facilitates the interaction between groups of IFF fellows and situations where inspiration is needed. He observes that the group does its best work when each individual turns up in a curious frame of mind, willing to learn: 'if even just one or two of those powerful individuals turns up full of their own learning, there's no room for anything else.' What this speaks to is the need for our work to be *embodied* in the sense that it requires each of us to 'be the change that we want to see in the world.' Consequently, our work also needs to be reflective. That is, we need to become increasingly self aware (aware of our own mindset and worldview), open to the need for new learning and the ability to understand other perspectives, and able to change our own practice in response.

New tools, implements, maps and frameworks can also help when we are grappling with the challenge of making sense of our circumstances. These frameworks can act as a trigger for transformational change. However, what we have observed in Andrew's work is a true integration between who he is and what he does. Consequently, his use of models/frameworks/tools is, above all, to facilitate a relationship with others so that they can talk about, frame and try to act reasonably to further life. The models, used in the abstract and separate from this motivation, are often sterile and unhelpful; in the abstract, they are separated from this motivation about life and pressed into the service of policy. This then leads to ugly terms like 'rolling out' and 'scaling up'.

So, in Andrew's practice, models and frameworks are a means to an end. One such framework is the 'world system model' developed by IFF member Tony Hodgson, represented opposite. We visited Tony on one of our learning journeys. His model is inspired by awareness of complexity and the danger of 'synchronous failure' that now afflicts us all. The world model creates zones which allow a more comprehensive view. The most important point is that each of the twelve zones interconnects and interacts with all the others. This is why we find such profound complexity.

In earlier chapters we considered the threats posed by climate, energy, water, food, well-being, habitat and biosphere. The zones in the world model also include wealth (inequalities are undermining social stability); governance (geopolitically inspired wars revolve around power and resources and make global solutions impossible to implement); community (eroded community coherence and passive dependency within an individualistic and competitive culture are degrading resilience); trade (the unintended side effects of our flawed version of globalisation are destroying

The IFF World System Model

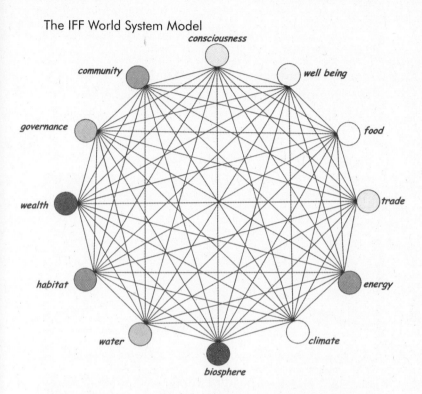

resilient local economies); and world view (fragmented ways of thinking – including the dominance of reductionism and specialisation – and multiple forms of fundamentalism are preventing the emergence of a shared, one planet living world view).

It follows that the emerging holistic paradigm that we need must be better suited to responding to the challenges of a highly interconnected world. The model has been used as the basis for a 'game' to help participants grapple in a coherent way with complexity. Andrew has also worked with Bruce Whyte at the Glasgow Centre for Population Health to create an interactive resource – Understanding Glasgow – which uses the same broad approach.

Another example of an IFF framework that can stimulate richer conversations about the present and facilitate new thinking about possibilities is the 'three horizons' framework. Each horizon possesses certain typical characteristics.

Horizon 1 (H1 in the diagram above) represents the current system or business as usual. It is under strain and beginning to show signs of failing and facing challenges of sustainability.

The Three Horizons

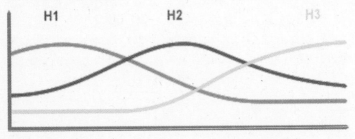

Horizon 3 (H3) represents a completely different, viable system, one adapted to new conditions, having taken 20 or 30 years, or more, to reach this stage. Horizon 2 (H2), however, represents the struggle between these two: the old system declining in importance and the new struggling to emerge. Horizon 2 represents the transition from one infrastructure to another.

Each Horizon is also associated with a particular mindset. In Horizon 1 the priority is to shore up the existing system, to 'keep the lights on': this mindset is likely to regard Third Horizon proponents as irrelevant and will seek to capture successful innovation in the Second Horizon in order to perpetuate the (failing) First Horizon system, often in the guise of 'scaling' successful experiments. The mindset of Horizon 2 is entrepreneurial. It senses the failings of Horizon 1 and opportunities to do things differently. But it faces a choice between using its ingenuity to shore up the old system or rather working to shift policy and practice towards the new model it glimpses in Horizon 3. Horizon 3 is the visionary mindset, seeing the first as misguided and the second as promising. It is driven by people who are acting from a basis of authenticity, values and belief. In practice such people are often sowing the seeds of a radically new future, usually 'under the radar' of the first. All three perspectives exist at the current time and have their advocates and their bodies of evidence. A policy option that has little to recommend it in the First Horizon may have a large part to play in a possible Third Horizon – and is therefore worth investing in as a Second Horizon innovation. The introduction of 'horizons thinking' formalises the recognition of at least three different worldviews, three simultaneous views of the present. Thinking in terms of horizons helps to create the change in consciousness that seems required by the scope and scale of the challenges presented.

This chapter has presented two individuals and their organisations: both are exploring new ways of thinking, being and doing. Each in their own way is helping to explore new 'maps' of reality. It is our contention, however, that the future will emerge through collective action – the activities of many and the new web of meaning that we create among ourselves. The solutions will be global and local and at all points in between. Therefore, the next chapter asks how we should each live in the face this complex challenge.

'Spending on the NHS has grown tenfold from £12 billion (2010 prices) in 1950 to £120 billion today.'

CHAPTER SEVEN
What next for a healthy Scotland?

The year after the NHS was established in 1948 saw an unprecedented number of hernia repairs preformed on working aged men. Why? – because prior to the provision of medical care which was 'free at the point of delivery' working men simply had to put up with their pathology. The history of the NHS is that of an organisation established after a century's discussion on the provision of health services to meet a long recognised need. It appeared at a time when Britain saw health care as crucial to one of the 'five giants' that the Beveridge Report declared should be slain during post-war reconstruction (want, disease, squalor, ignorance, idleness). The cataclysm of war provided an opportunity that might not have been taken in quieter times.

The NHS was noble in conception: based on an integration of 'the true', 'the good' and 'the beautiful'. The idea that human beings naturally integrate the true, the good and the beautiful comes originally from Plato. If we apply it to the NHS we see that arguments in 1948 based simply on empirical evidence (the true) were necessary but not sufficient. There was massive unmet health care need and the state was able to respond – but that had been true for a very long time and that truth on its own had not been sufficient to bring about change. The true needed support from the good – an ethical argument about fairness. Social justice demanded that a wealthy nation like the UK should not deny cost effective health care to all. Yet, we know that, despite the moral power of that argument, many countries today (including the USA) still exclude those who cannot pay from many important aspects of health care. A third force was needed: we are calling this 'the beautiful' – that which fires our imaginations and raises our consciousness. The NHS came into existence in 1948, and not before, because it took the great interwar depression followed by the social upheavals of World War II to change the consciousness of the British people. It simply seemed inconceivable to men and women from all social classes who had served together, and thus become aware of each other in a new way, that Britain could return after the war to being the same class-ridden society. The collective consciousness had changed. So, it was the integration of arguments that were true (evidence), good (social justice) and beautiful (the imagination that comes from a change in consciousness) that gave rise to the post-war welfare state and the NHS.

Interestingly, the people who worked in the NHS and those that used it during those early decades shared the consciousness that helped create it: the NHS was seen as a collective resource that should be used wisely. At first, resources were scarce and waiting lists long but tolerance and patience matched these shortcomings. However, with the rise of consumerism, the consciousness that informed decisions about our NHS changed. More resources were provided from which many benefitted but the ethos, in time, became consumerist and econometric. Thus, in recent decades we have seen experiments in the NHS internal market, the patient's charter, and target setting. These new forces have created a health service that is modern and technically sophisticated but it is not sustainable.

It is not sustainable financially. Spending on the NHS has grown tenfold from £12 billion (2010 prices) in 1950 to £120 billion today. The economy has grown during this time too, but not at an equivalent rate. At its inception in 1948 the proportion of GDP spent on the NHS was 3%; now it is 9%. The rising trend shows no signs of weakening: quite the opposite. The NHS is likely to face significant pressures in the next few years as a consequence of an ageing population, rising staff costs and new technologies.

It is not sustainable 'emotionally'. Staff report feeling alienated, stressed and disenfranchised. Patients report mixed reaction but a constant theme is the sense of being, at times, like a cog in a highly complex machine.

These observations mirror arguments we have been making throughout this book. Modernity is no longer sustainable – ecologically, economically or emotionally. In response, we will need, once again, to integrate the true, the good and the beautiful. Yet, an integral approach is difficult for us because we are so influenced by modernity. It is, for example, a maxim of public health that we need to make the healthy choices the easy choices: we need healthy public policy, supportive social structures and nurturing organisations if individuals in Scotland are to be healthier. For this reason, debates about what next for a healthy Scotland tend to focus on policies and structures. What we are suggesting is that policies and structures are inseparable from the consciousness that created them.

Current thinking assumes that continuing economic growth within current structures will fund new technologies that will allow us to engineer a solution which will keep most aspects of our lives intact (e.g. consumption, commuting, energy utilisation) and solve the problems created by the dis-eases of modernity and our lack of sustainability. The flaw in this set of expectations is that our economy depends on the natural world for resources and ecological services. The big question, therefore, is whether we can develop technologies that allow consumption to continue on its current growth trajectory in the face of an expanding global population? Current evidence suggests that the levels of technological improvement that will be needed are huge and not something we have ever experienced before. Alternatively, we may have to consider different forms of economic arrangements that allow human needs to be met within ecological constraints.

Our conclusion is that, while technological improvement will be essential, there will be considerable reductions in the level of and changes in the nature of our consumption in Scotland. Conventional economic growth will either stop because we create another model or it will collapse due to ecological and economic pressures. These forces are now inevitable. We cannot know the timing but what we can be certain about is the inevitability of the need to reduce consumption radically (or, at least, change the current model of consumption).

So, how do we respond in the face of this reality – this

statement of 'the true'? One obvious response has to do with 'the good' – an ethical response. We must support the vulnerable in our society across the whole life course. A baby is born fully dependent on others for all his or her needs. However, the baby will, if healthy, outgrow this phase of development, become a toddler, then, in turn, a child, an adolescent, young adult and so on. Failure to navigate one of the stages of development can have severe consequences. For example, failure to bond with a parent can impede healthy development, hamper the ability to form empathetic relation-ships and may lead to violence and mental ill health in later life. Another example is when lack of employment makes it difficult for adolescents to find a place in the adult world: antisocial behaviour, teenage pregnancy, gang culture and much else can result. So, even as it is changing, our Scottish society needs to ensure that there are effective means to ensure that all children pass healthily through all life stages and that adults are supported as they make their many transitions. Family, kinship groups and the broader society through a variety of structures like schools, workplaces and clubs have historically provided these support structures. Importantly, religious traditions have also played a part in this process. It is commonplace to observe that many of these supports have been eroded. What we need now are ways to rebuild some of what we have lost and the inventiveness to create new structures where they are needed. The latter flows from what we are calling 'the beautiful' – imagination that is fired and consciousness that is raised.

Unfortunately, our political system is set up to deal with the short term and uses the tools of modernity to solve the problems created by modernity. For example, our current economic model constantly needs to create extra demand for goods and services. To pay for this demand there is a need for credit and, to service the debt, an excess return must be generated (above the cost of that debt). This spiral of growing debt and money supply is built into the economic system. For example, the achievement of economic growth is still the Scottish Government's top objective and the insertion of the word 'sustainable' before 'economic' does not hide the intrinsically econometric nature of this target.

The argument that has been used to support the current approach is that as long as the economy grows, the debt will (eventually) be repaid. However, pursuit of economic growth in the UK in recent decades has led to widening inequalities and has been accompanied by the emergence of an amoral culture which has brought us to the edge of financial collapse. The current growth of debt in the West cannot be combated by standard macro-economic interventions because economic growth is running up against ecological constraints. It costs more energy to extract energy, global warming exacts a cost, depleting resources become more expensive and exhausted through over exploitation. Yet, our political leaders continue to give the impression that they can and should nurse our global financial system back into (perpetual) growth. People may pray that they are right: they hope against hope that the world can go back to how it was. Yet, in our hearts, most of us seem to realise that the system is inherently unstable and unsustainable and, as a consequence, we fear for the future and lose confidence in our politicians.

Some 'greens' give the impression that complete collapse of the current system would almost be desirable. As public health professionals we know that economic shocks destroy health, as was seen in the health trends of the population in the former Soviet Union following the collapse of communism, the depression in the United States during the 1920s, and with Scottish de-industrialisation in the 1970s and 1980s. What this teaches us is that there are a great number of benefits associated with modernity that we will want to preserve. Our favourite example is anaesthetic dentistry – but the list is long. Much of what we know of the modern world needs to be preserved but in a modified form. James Lovelock describes this as a strategic retreat from the excesses of modernity. We need plans to maintain our food supply, ensure that we can produce a reasonable amount of renewable energy and manufacture essential goods for our own consumption and for export. In short, we will need to provide for ourselves: after all, even Robinson Crusoe had to pick fruit, catch fish and milk the goat.

Scotland will have to pay its way in an increasingly competitive global economy. Consequently, we should honour those in our society who are entrepreneurial and develop a wide range of policy innovations that help to make the transition possible. We will need an ethical imperative to make sure that change happens fairly (fair to all of our own population, all the citizens of the world and to unborn generations to come). We will also need imagination and creativity to nourish these changes.

The frightening truth is that our government has hardly begun this task. The trouble is that the actions that are needed will require a degree of courage that our political system tends not to reward. The evidence of history is that our politicians are only as brave as we give them permission to be: for example, it was only when it became clear that the public in Scotland would support a smoking ban in public places that the measure was introduced. We know from personal experience that the idea had been floated with politicians many times in previous years but it always seemed 'too risky' until the population got behind it. This example suggests that, as citizens, we need to help our politicians to be brave.

What kinds of policies could change our economy and social structures? This is a good question because, if we consider the NHS in 1948 as an example, it emerged from a changed consciousness but its subsequent success also helped win over those who did not at first support a state health service. What kind of policy might arise out of our changing conscious-ness which would also fire the imaginations of those who are trapped in denial or depression?

We hesitate to make any suggestion but the following example does illustrate where a debate about policy might begin. Consider the citizen's income. Currently, our benefits system can create dependency and is marred by poverty traps. Let us imagine an alternative. Let us imagine that a Scottish government introduces a Citizen's Income (CI) – that is, an unconditional, non-withdrawable income payable to each individual as a right of citizenship. It would need to be relatively generous to work and, because the Citizen's Income is not withdrawn as earnings rise, a large CI would mean that net income would rise steadily for the poorest families as earned income rises. For flexible workers, a Citizen's Income would provide a measure of security on which they could build. This would allow people to develop more flexible patterns of working more consistent with their own and their children's or other dependents' needs. Thus, consistently higher levels of employment might be expected. A Citizen's Income could help people to undertake higher education, training, or retraining by providing a small, secure income.

At present it is difficult to imagine such a policy getting off the ground. It attracts interest but it would require higher taxation to pay for an adequately generous CI, so it lacks widespread support. That is because it is considered mostly from the perspective of what is 'true'. If we could integrate what is 'true' with emerging visions of the 'good' and the 'beautiful', new possibilities would open up.

Citizen's income is just one of a multitude of policies that may be needed to create a healthier and fairer Scotland. Other examples include an individual carbon allocation, an integrated transport network, active commuting policies and a food policy that promotes health, wealth and sustainability.

However, policy-induced structural change on its own is never enough: Scotland has some of the most ambitious climate change targets in the world. Does that mean that the population of Scotland is changing its world view and behaviours? We will leave the reader to answer that question.

We sense that, to meet the challenge of decarbonising our way of life, the emerging culture will embrace voluntary simplicity: using less stuff and becoming more local and self-sufficient. Note, we should move forward towards this future – it is not a return to a pre-technological age. The good news is that there is considerable evidence to suggest that voluntary simplicity could improve our well-being. Consider the up side: many will jump off the hedonic treadmill; choice anxiety will be reduced; physical activity will increase as we walk and cycle more; we will grow more for ourselves and spend more time in simple activities that relate to other people; voluntary simplicity will reduce inequalities and change the symbolic meaning of consumption. It is impossible to predict the detail of this but our main point is that much that is beneficial could emerge from a new culture.

On the other hand, if we are forced into change – if it is not voluntary – we are likely to experience a heightened sense of loss. We know that a focus on constraints, shortage and failure closes the human mind down – it narrows our repertoire of responses and inhibits creativity. Therefore, we need to consider what resources are abundant. These include: life itself; the creativity and diversity of nature; the capacity of our bodies to heal and regenerate; human ingenuity; our capacity to learn; the pleasure we take in each other; our capacity for compassion. . . and much more.

By focusing on abundance, we broaden our imaginations and help each other build creative responses. Evidence from well-being studies simply confirms what our wisdom traditions have known for generations – individual happiness is not an end in itself. We are truly happy when we find engaging activity with a sense of purpose and meaning and exercise our gifts in the service of others. We know that relationships matter more than things and that to be happy we need to meet basic needs – not all wants. Life is living through us – we are all connected and part of a greater whole. Awareness that we are all expressions of some deeper unity fosters compassion and care for others and our world.

It is possible to think of such a world emerging because we

know that cultures can and do change. To understand how cultures change it may be helpful to think about seminal events in history that have left an indelible mark on our consciousness. One of the most significant of these in the evolution of modernity was Galileo's observation that the earth moved round the sun and not the other way round. This discovery came at a particular time in our history, when the technology was available (telescope) along with a growing mass of astronomical data that increasingly challenged the underlying assumptions of the earth-centric worldview. What had limited our ability to grasp this way of seeing the world previously was less our lack of imagination and more a product of the culture, which made the Catholic Church the final arbiter of truth. In Galileo's time many scientists, philosophers and theologians were beginning to challenge this hegemony. He simply would not have been able to conceive his ideas and theories in the absence of dissent from other quarters. The reaction to his findings was typical of a culture challenged by discoveries that undermine its deeply held worldview. There was shock, denial and renunciation. The problem was that new insights about what is 'true' (the earth is not the centre of the universe) threatened the medieval underpinning of the 'good' (the authority of the church which saw the earth at the centre of a universe created by God) and what is 'beautiful' (the idea of the geocentric, symmetrical universe).

However, a few brave individuals looked at the evidence set out by Galileo and his calculations, which were subsequently improved by Kepler, and began to accept the implications, not just rationally, but emotionally. Importantly, these pioneers naturally developed an integral approach to what was true, good and beautiful and allowed each perspective to develop without threatening the other. This is one of the great achievements of modernity as it allowed science, ethics and aesthetics to develop unimpeded by constraints.

The problem was that, by the time we reach the more recent manifestation of modernity, the 'true' (a narrow view of evidence and science) has been allowed to overshadow the 'good' and the 'beautiful'. During our learning journeys we heard many versions of the same complaint: that our society only values one type of knowledge (narrowly defined scientific evidence) and places value on money and economic outcomes above all others. We have already argued that science as a method is invaluable but when it morphs into a system of beliefs and values it is more appropriately called 'scientism' (an ideology). Equally, economics is a useful tool but when we elevate economics above all other perspectives we are again dealing with an ideology – 'economism'. The way in which we have fallen under the tyranny of scientism and economism is another example of how initially beneficial aspects of modernity have been carried too far.

The inner and outer worlds of a modern Scot are radically different from those of a pre-modern person or an individual from a different contemporary culture. Yet, most people in Scotland today behave as if their own world view and the way we organise out society is somehow 'natural' or the 'only way it could be'. The dominant world view of modernity is that a human being is a biological machine – the product of chance and time set in a universe made up of particles that interact in a manner that allows us to understand how the universe works and predict what will happen when we intervene. As our bodies are biological machines we simply need to understand how to fix them when they malfunction. We conceptualise our world as a place of plenty (without functional limits) which we can exploit to meet our needs. We are not arguing that people believe these ideas simplistically or uncritically. Nonetheless, much of what happens in our current trajectory is the product of this world view.

However, amongst people we have met who are engaged in transformational change, a new story is emerging. People find the vocabulary difficult but express themselves in statements like: 'a possible way forward is to see ourselves as part of the Life Force, which has been unfolding since time began as a means of knowing itself: we are not simply the products of chance and time.' People sense that we are part of the web of life but are different from animals because we have a more conscious appreciation: we have greater powers of co-creation with the Life Force than animals and plants. This position is different from a purely materialist evolutionary perspective and from an orthodox religious point of view. What people seem to be grasping for is the idea that the capacity to create complexity, to develop or to evolve seems to be an intrinsic quality of our universe and we, as humans, have become aware of this. Other people at other times in their own cultures have attributed this unfolding to a divine being or beings. In contrast, modernity insists there is nothing beyond matter, chance and time.

We need to be humble in the face of these arguments (perhaps better described as mysteries). We are not just a node on the web of life. We are a node on the web of life and a wonderful one at that. We are self aware and aware of the universe. Daniel Dennett has said, 'it is as if the universe has grown a nervous system and we are it'. We need to appreciate better and marvel at the workings of the human body and of our universe. Making space for wonder seems important because it allows us to go beyond our narrowly defined problems. At the same time, we also need to appreciate that we are part of the biosphere and subject to all the constraints that implies. We are not special in the sense that we are exempt from the constraints of ecology. We have no guaranteed destiny: The future is radically open.

If we are to move beyond the world view that created our current crisis, time and attention will be needed. Each will choose their own technique. For some, contemplation while enjoying nature works best: for others, mindfulness practice or contemplative prayer. Some will take a more cerebral approach (e.g. reading and discussion) while others will be more intuitive (e.g. journeys with a purpose) or mystical (e.g. Eastern forms of meditation). The point is that each of us needs time and discipline to explore our inner world and develop in a way that is coherent with the emerging age.

Each of us must take responsibility for our own thoughts and actions. This is healthy individualism. At the same time we need the wisdom that can come from interaction with others. Indeed, most of us will want to be part of a group or community which helps us take effective action. None of us wants to be defined by the collective but we do want the fellowship of others. This tension – between healthy individualism and a desire for community – is part of what we discovered on our learning journeys throughout Scotland.

Our recommendation is that we learn to better integrate the true, the good and the beautiful. We hear people argue that 'we must start with policies that redistribute wealth and power'. This is countered by 'the only thing I can change is myself'. A third will say 'we need to change the culture of Scotland first' while the fourth says 'if it's a crisis, it's up to individuals to 'just do it'.' The point is that we need all of the above and more – not acting independently or sequentially but integrally. This ability to think and act integrally will be a key twenty-first century competence.

The critique of modernity articulated in this book does not mean that economic growth will not continue in the short term or that progress will not continue to be made in many aspects of our lives. What it does imply is that our current economic model is not sustainable and our culture is no longer underpinned by a widespread confidence in the ideas of 'progress' and 'growth' that gave it such initial energy. The three horizon model of the International Futures Forum is helpful in this context. Remember, the three horizons are not time horizons (short, medium and long-term): rather they are ways of thinking/being/doing that co-exist in all time frames.

As we stand in the present, we can recognise the presence of all three horizons. The first horizon dominates at present but the third horizon is emergent. Also, we can only really innovate in the second horizon as the third is still beyond our view and we do not know how this is going to take shape. However, with a third horizon in mind, we can innovate in a different way – using the creative energy of innovation to help the third horizon into being, rather than allowing that energy to be sucked into keeping the existing system going for just a little bit longer.

The lesson of history is that we should be hopeful. It must have been tough for our earliest ancestors in the African forests when the climate changed and the grasslands spread, forcing them to find a new way to sustain themselves. Yet, that hardship forced our ancestors to learn how to survive on grassland that led in time to the 'out of Africa' migration and subsequent populating of the rest of the world by early humans. Equally, it must have been difficult to develop agricultural techniques and the domestication of animals for the first time so that larger groupings of humans could be fed. By the same token, we have already observed how traumatising it was for crofters to be pulled off the land and into factories when the industrial revolution started. Yet, each of these transitions represented an important chapter in human history. Each transition brought in new ways of living which brought many benefits. That, we hope, is what's next for a healthy Scotland'. ☐

OTHER TITLES IN THIS SERIES

The Great Takeover: How materialism, the media and markets now dominate our lives

Carol Craig

ISBN:978 1 908931061 £5.99

This book describes the dominance of materalist values, the media and business in all our lives and how this is leading to a loss of individual and collective well-being. It looks at many of the big issues of our times – debt, inequality, political apathy, loss of self-esteem, pornography and the rise of celebrity culture. The conclusion is simple and ultimately hopeful – we can change our values and our lives.

Carol Craig is Chief Executive of the Centre for Confidence and Well-being which she established in 2004. She is author of *The Scots' Crisis of Confidence* (2003 and 2011); *Creating Confidence: A handbook for professionals working with young people* (2007); and *The Tears that Made the Clyde: Well-being in Glasgow* (2010).

The New Road: charting Scotland's inspirational communities

Alf Young and Ewan Young

ISBN:978 1 908931078 £5.99

A father and son go on a week long journey round Scotland to see at first hand some of the great environmental, social, employment and regeneration projects which are happening round the country. From Dunbar in the south east of Scotland to Knoydart in the north west they meet people involved in projects which demonstrate new ways of living.

Alf Young writes, broadcasts and comments on a range of issues affecting Scotland and the wider world. He retired in 2009 from the *Herald* where he was responsible for comment and opinion. He writes a Saturday column for the *Scotsman* and is a regular contributor to BBC current affairs programmes. Currently chairman of Riverside Inverclyde and of Social Investment Scotland, he is also an economic adviser to the Scottish Council for Development and Industry.

Ewan Young works as Development Officer for the Ullapool Community Trust. Sustainable living is one of his passions. Holding degreess in Planning and Environmental Sustainability, he lives near Ulapool with his wife, Merlin.

FORTHCOMING TITLE IN THIS SERIES

Throwing Doves at the Moon: a radical rethinking of management
Tony Miller and Gordon Hall

ISBN:978 1 908931 14 6 £5.99

Scotland's technically advanced, modern society is still not what it could be. There are chronic problems that continue to haunt us, problems that defy our decision makers, both in the public and private sectors.

This book considers the flawed assumptions that underpin our management practice; how they block our progress and cause significant waste, especially of our people's potential. It brings together ideas that could revolutionise the way we think of management and provide a way forward for Scotland. Miller & Hall argue that management's approach to controlling large organisations is futile; well past its sell-by date. A radical alternative is proposed based on restoring the individual, on recognising the role of community within organisations, and redefining the role of managers in complex organisations.

[over]

Tony Miller is an electrical engineer by training. He retired recently from Robert Gordon University He was a member of the Deming Learning Network, based in Aberdeen.

Gordon Hall Gordon is the CEO of the Deming Learning Network in Aberdeen. He has identified with encouraging the search for knowledge in the context of management. Coming from a systems perspective he is particularly interested in how we cooperate within organisations and across society as a whole. He initiated a group known as the Unreasonable Learners, whose basic aim is to seek cooperation amongst the many forward thinkers across Scotland. Their web site is www.unreasonable-learners.com.

Move over!

By Janine Amos and Annabel Spenceley
Consultant Rachael Underwood

CHERRYTREE BOOKS

A Cherrytree Book

Designed and produced
by A S Publishing

Copyright this edition © Evans Brothers Ltd 2003
First published in 1999
by Cherrytree Books
a division of the Evans Publishing Group
2A Portman Mansions
Chiltern St
London W1U 6NR

First published in paperback 2003. Reprinted 2004

British Library Cataloguing in Publication Data

Amos, Janine
    Move over!. – (Good friends)
    1.Friendship – Pictorial works – Juvenile literature
    I. Title II.Annabel Spenceley
    302.3'4

ISBN 1 84234 156 1

Printed and bound in Malaysia

The tent

Farid's in the tent.

Here comes Lily.

Farid and Lily are in the tent.

Here come Jack and Ceri.

Farid and Lily and Jack and Ceri are all
in the tent.

Here comes Sam.

Sam squeezes into the tent.
How do the others feel?

"Move over!" grumbles Jack.
"I'm squashed."

"And I'm squashed," says Lily.
"This tent is too small."

Lily crawls out.

Lily gets two chairs.

"I need this rug," she says.
"Help me, Sam."

Lily and Sam make another tent.

Now there's room for everyone.

Oh dear! Here comes Peter!

The rocket

The table is covered with boxes.
Jamie is building a rocket.

20

"Hey! Move over! I need more space,"
says Nathan.

"Zoom! Zoom!" goes Jamie.

"Move over!" shouts Nathan.
He pushes the boxes on to the floor.

"You two look upset," says Steve.
"What's going on?"

"Nathan pushed my boxes," says Jamie.

"He's taking up all the table.
There's no room for me," says Nathan.

"So you both need more space,"
says Steve. "What can we do?"

"I've got a good idea," says Jamie.
"I could build my model up."

"Show me!" says Steve.
Jamie tips his rocket up.

29

"Look! There's space for me now!"
smiles Nathan.

Jamie finishes his rocket.
And Nathan makes his model.

People need space to work and play.
Sometimes they haven't got enough room.
They feel cramped and they get angry.

If you need more space, stop and look around.
Perhaps you can find a way to make the space
you need.
You might want to ask another person to help you.